Life is a Dance

And God is the Choreographer

Cheryl Lynn Smith

Life is a Dance

And God is the Choreographer

Cheryl Lynn Smith

Psalm 149:3 "Let them praise His Name with dance."

Cheryl Lynn Smith

© 2023

Editor: Deborah Hamilton
Cover Photo: Trinity Walker Keefer
Model: Rachael Scott
Contributor: Mariah Henry

Introduction

This is one of the hardest things in life I have ever done. Me? Write a book? An inspirational memoir? No way! I have a tough enough time trying to speak using the right words, nevertheless, write. The inception of my book began in 2008 and the delivery - 15 years later!

It all began at the Outer Banks, North Carolina, on the third floor of a friend's beach home. Gazing out at the ocean, serenaded by the waves and basking in the beautiful September breeze; I was captivated by the providence of God surrounding me.

After many years as a born-again Christian, I still knew so little about God. I am forever learning more about God than my mind or heart often feels it can handle. Throughout this book, mainly my life's journey, I hope you will be able to identify 'life as a dance.' Ultimately, even though we want to dance when we want to, the way we want to and how we want to, God is the designer and choreographer of the dance, the way He wants, how He wants and for HIS GLORY.

Acknowledgements & Thanks

I want to thank everyone who has ever been a part of the dance God has designed for my life; special family members and friends who have journeyed with me along my daily dance. Loving thanks goes to my husband Gary (my life-journey partner and friend), who always holds me to the Word of God, a higher standard of living. Gratitude goes to my family, Nicole & Mike, Matthew & Skye and Joshua, who have been the best teachers throughout all the seasons of my life and the dispensers of many of my life joys; our special treasures (grandchildren) - Ocean, Isaiah, Azalea and Nova; my dad & mom, Philip and Janet Kyte (home in Heaven), to whom I am forever thankful for allowing me the privilege to dance from the age of three until I married at age nineteen. They sacrificed many luxuries in life. I'll always be grateful to my grandmother, Madeline Carter, who introduced me to the church (Fort Howard Community Church) where Gary and I gave our lives to Christ and served for five years. We will always be grateful to our dear friend, Harry Iman, who was an encouraging support in our Christian lives from the day I trusted in Christ and forward, until the day Harry left earth to be forever with the Lord.

I owe an extreme amount of gratitude to my dance instructor, Jean Kettell, for the privilege to excel in dance and for teaching me how to choreograph. She believed in me! She played such a big part in my life, because I lived at the dance studio four nights a week and Saturdays.

Thanks to all my friends. Tosha – a dancing friend who has stuck by me through thick and thin, and I mean that literally, or should I say physically as a dancer; thanks for picking up my diploma – you know what I mean! Joyce Ann, my longest childhood friend who was first to venture into dance with me; thanks! "Banana-banana" - an inside joke! Thanks to Deb Hamilton, who came into my life unexpectedly (via Betsy Beck), who took my book and walked with me through each chapter, edited and encouraged me to tell my story! Dr. Frank and Flo Simansky (home in Heaven) -thanks for always being there for me at any given moment and for the freedom to use your beach home in the Outer Banks of North Carolina (nearest place to Heaven on earth) for family vacations, resting and writing. Gratitude, always, to my Church Family, who have encouraged me to pen my life's story.

Special thanks goes to my sister, Tanya, who has always gone the extra mile for my family and me; Joe and Cindy, my brother-in-law and sister-in-law and their family, who have played an instrumental role in our family dance! They have walked with us along all the roads we've traveled since 1975.

To all my dance students who have given me immense fulfillment and joy watching them transform into dancers before my eyes, sparkling with pride. You're the best!

Lastly, but actually first, my greatest thanks goes to God, Who has been so very patient with me to follow His lead once again. I am humbled by His pursuing me with His everlasting love and believing in me to write this book. May He use this for His eternal purpose! And, may all who read this be blessed and DANCE!

"The LORD bless you and keep you; The LORD make His face shine upon you, and be gracious to you; The LORD lift up His countenance upon you, and give you peace." (Numbers 6:24-25)

This book is dedicated to all who have ever danced and those who have always wanted to!

Contents

1
Born to Dance

———————————————————

Where are you in your story of life?
Can you trust God to take the pen and finish writing it?

"God is still writing your story; quit trying to steal the pen. Trust the Author."
(Author Unknown)

Growing up in a rowhome (predecessor to the modern townhome) in Baltimore, Maryland, where the community consisted of workers from General Motors, Bethlehem, Eastern and Thompson Steel Mills and Western Electric, our blue-collared neighborhood was a melting pot; a diversity of many ethnic groups. Neighbors became like close-knit families. It was just commonplace to borrow a stick of butter or eggs from your next-door neighbors. We needed each other and shared everyday life.

The games we played as kids were a part of exploring life: tin-can alley, hopscotch, rubber band jump rope, riding bicycles with baseball cards attached with clothes pins to the wheels, adjustable metal roller skates with keys, hide 'n seek and most exciting was the Whirlybird! I was the only child in all of West Inverness who had the Whirlybird play equipment. It housed four metal seats with a bar to pull back and push forward, making the ride spin faster and faster. Needless to say, I had more 'new' friends every week!

Backtracking a little, just out of my toddler years, who could have guessed that my life would be forever changed by simply walking past a dance studio at the age of just three years old? My mom and I were strolling down a strip mall sidewalk, when my attention was completely seized and smitten by the sound of music and my first remembrance of my eyes catching sight of... *dancers!* Stopping abruptly in my tracks to watch through the inviting window pane, as I pressed my face to the glass in wonder, I knew at age three - *I wanted to dance!* My mom enrolled me in ballet and the story begins.

As the years clicked by, I ventured into other forms of dance such as jazz, pointe and tap. The love of all dancing for me, though, was tap. I seemed to pick up the steps naturally and with utter ease.

I now had a second home – the dance studio. The mirrors, leotards, costumes, ballet shoes, tap shoes and music all percolated pure excitement. Dance was what I lived for!

Dance filled a need in my life. It was a daily therapy. Not that I thought I needed it, but I loved how it filled me with peace, joy and exhilaration. I loved to perform on stage. I loved to perform before an audience of two, my parents in our living room, or thousands at the Civic Center with Bob Hope. Compliments spurred me on to greater depths of accomplishment. My family support was a constant sacrifice.

Special childhood memories in my *dance of life* involve our annual family getaway vacations. Get out your map! I specifically remember trips to the Catskill Mountains in New York where I first experienced pistachio ice cream – yummy! We traveled to popular tourist sites like Ocean City, Maryland, where we settled into our temporary vacation quarters, the Tahiti Motel, and then ventured on to the Wildwood Crest at the Diamond Beach Resort, a private beach community in New Jersey. Back in the 1960s and 70s, one-week vacations were the norm for most families. Now, in the 21st century, it seems families take many short trips during long weekends.

Our vacation highlight came but once a year. As an only child for eleven years, bundling up in the backseat of the car in the wee morning hours with a blanket and pillow was roomy, warm and welcoming. Even though my parents thought I would sleep at that time of night while they navigated dark roads destined for ocean and fun, the butterflies of excitement in my stomach were simply too intense. So, my squirrelly little head would pop up and ask the questions imbedded into every child's genes, "Are we there yet?" and "How much longer?" Can you feel my anticipation?

A local highlight in my early youth was when my dad surprised me with tickets to go to the "Bozo the Clown" show at WJZ-TV in Baltimore. And, as so many things in my childhood centered around dance, that is where I learned to dance the Lorenzo Stomp!

Oh! I almost forgot! I can put down in my resume of life that I experienced firsthand the adventures of camping. Although one is NOT 'roughing it' in a motorhome with air conditioning, and all meals prepared beforehand, and the night ritual of sitting around a fire, it still technically qualifies as camping. I never did favor camping after that (ha-ha). But when I journeyed to Haiti on my missionary trip later in life, I was thrust into real-life 'roughing-it' camping. (I'll share more about that in another chapter.)

Vacations wove such wonderful memories for me as a child, resulting in my husband, Gary, and me continuing the vacation tradition as our children entered our lives. We took our one-year-old daughter, Nicole, to Lancaster, Pennsylvania, to experience the Amish community with horses and buggies. Proud daddy just had to buy a homemade Amish bonnet for his little girl. The price: $25.00. Ouch! That was a lot of money in 1983. Our various vacations took us to a cabin on a lake in Albany, New York; to Williamsburg, Virginia, for the history; to a Condo in West Palm Beach, Florida; to Beaver Creek in Vail, Colorado, which was provided free through a family who blesses pastors in ministry; to Dallas, Texas, to stay with our friends, the Swifts; to Washington, DC, for the Cherry Blossom Festival and to the Outer Banks, North Carolina, at the beach home of our friends, Frank and Flo. Our family vacationed at the Outer Banks almost every year for rest and relaxation watching the waves, the horses on the beach, and just good old sun-time fun.

But, the most memorable of all was an all-expense paid trip to Orlando Florida with my mom, dad, my sister Tanya, her husband and our family of five. Disney World, Epcot, River Country and Universal are stamped on our minds with never-ending, warm memories! Thanks, Mom and Dad! These are vacation highlights we experienced as a family, which sliced out special time for us to draw closer to each other. For that I am forever grateful!

I remember so many wonderful times with my mom and dad. Mom was very pleasantly surprised when she gave birth to me, since she had been told that she may never have any children due to female issues with which she was diagnosed.

Ten years later, my mom was scheduled for a hysterectomy and admitted to the hospital the night before the procedure. Very distressful news occurred simultaneously when her father was admitted to the very same hospital with an internal hemorrhage. Most sadly, her father passed away that night, so she ended up leaving the hospital, returning home and rescheduling the operation.

Several weeks later, when she went to the hospital for the pre-op procedures for her rescheduled surgery, she was told they needed to run a routine pregnancy test to make sure she was not pregnant. Mom just laughed at that unnecessary test! Well! Well! Well! She was going to have to go home *again* from the hospital with no scheduled operation. The blood test confirmed mom was miraculously pregnant! God has a way of changing our dance even when doctors think it is not possible.

Boy, was I ever thrilled when mom found out that she was pregnant and I was going to have a brother or a sister! I was definitely a spoiled child and everyone knew it — even me. So, when I asked at Christmastime, "Is that all?" after several packages had already been opened, *there was the proof!* I excitedly welcomed and was blessed with my little sister, Tanya, whose addition now created a stronger feeling of family. My dance was now about to change.

By the time I was a teenager, I lived at the dance studio five days a week. Practicing and performing became my way of life. It was a *magnificent obsession*. Though I was only 15, the privilege was presented to me to teach tap at the Jean Kettell Studio of Dance and Ballet/Tap at two recreation councils: Edgemere and West Inverness in Baltimore. This allowed me to develop my choreography skills. There is nothing like hearing music and being inspired to design a dance with many students in synchronization. Through all my stages of growing up, I was trying to reach my goal, my ambition and my dream of one day becoming a New York Radio City Music Hall Rockette.

2
My Dance of Love

An unforeseen, but delightful change crept up on me at 15 when I met my Prince Charming, Gary. When he walked into my life, my focus shifted. I fell hard and fast in love with him. One day, while I was babysitting my sister, Tanya, who was four at the time, Gary happened to pull his father's butter-colored Chrysler 300 into my backyard. Gary was actually looking for my friend, Cindy, who was at my home at the time.

When he approached my house, I was hoping he was there for me. When our eyes first locked, I had an immediate crush on him. His blonde hair, rosy cheeks and tall slender build absolutely captivated me. Gary told me, much later, that after he saw me at the door, he heard in his head, "You're going to marry that girl!"

Gary came inside and was interested in taking Cindy on a date, but she actually dodged him. I kept thinking to myself, *if she isn't interested, I am!* Cindy confided in me that she was not going out with Gary. Oh-yeah! That was my opportunity. I spoke up and said I would go out with him.

After Gary left the house that evening, he drove to a pay phone (Remember them?) and asked if he could return to my home and see me. I was *heart-leaping, beside-myself* surprised! He was as interested in me as I was in him.

We began dating that very night and after only three days he approached my mom, who had just come home from the hospital after having exploratory surgery, to ask if we could begin dating. He wanted to give me a ring (steady rings were a big thing back then). My mom and dad weren't too keen on a guy giving me, a tenth-grader, a ring after only three days. (This - I can totally understand now after having three children of my own.) Well, come to find out, I discovered at the lunch table in high school that the ring had been his former girlfriend's. Oh, oh, oh, oh, NO! Very bad idea! Not a good beginning to our relationship. I told him to take it back and I would be willing to wait for a new ring. Fast forward - three months later he gave me a different ring on my 16th birthday. That's better.

Not too long after I turned 16, I decided I was old enough to make the decision to show my love to Gary. When I think back, being so immature about giving up my gift of virginity at such a young age, I could cry. It was my choice and I still regret it! You can only give your virginity away one time. You will always remember where, when and with whom it happens. This is a part of my testimony I have shared in public schools, church youth groups, Lancaster Bible College, parent forums and homeschool networks through a group called 'One Ministries.' (I will introduce you to 'One' in a later chapter.)

To continue, I actually broke up with Gary about a year later. While we were apart, though, I felt a tugging to want to get back together. Little did I know then about a chemical called Oxytocin. This chemical is placed in our brain by God as the element which bonds us to the person with whom we are to spend the rest of our lives. This chemical is released in us when there is any physical affection and/or sexual intercourse.

Oxytocin* is released most when we engage in our first sexual intercourse. God intended us to experience this intimacy on our wedding night. Therefore, we would bond most to the person we give ourselves to in marriage. God planned to fuse us together by this chemical so we would remain together. Oxytocin is also released when a woman nurses a baby to bond her to her child.

After being apart almost six months, it was like a magnet pulling me back to Gary. We had been each other's first. We came back together and began to pick up right where we left off, intimacy and all.

Now, at 17, I had a once-in-a-lifetime audition at Radio City Music Hall in New York City for the Rockettes. Before I left to go to New York, my boyfriend, Gary, said to me, "I love you. I want to marry you. But if you make the audition, I will not wait for you. I lost you once before and do not want to lose you again." Those were heavy words to lay on a girl to think about on a four-hour ride from Baltimore where I lived, to New York City. This was the era before cell phones! No mobile communications.

My dance instructor, Jean, had set up the private audition, because of her connections having been a former Rockette. Upon arrival at the colossal Radio City Music Hall in New York, Violet Holmes, a former Rockette, Choreographer and Director, gave me a tour of Radio City. There truly is a city behind the stage you see from the seats in the theater. The audition lasted about an hour and, afterward, I felt confident that I did well.

So, do you think I passed the audition? Absolutely! I did! Do you think I went to New York? Nope. I decided to go back to Baltimore and get married. It was not an easy decision at all, but there were several factors that played into my decision-making dilemma.

In 1977, Radio City Music Hall fell into bankruptcy and this was the first time it was ever threatened with that problem. But in 1978, the year I married, it was restored to its former glory! Hmm . . . God? Next, the job would require me to take on two additional employments to supplement my income to make enough money to cover the cost of the apartment I would need to share with two other women. At this young age, almost 18, I just didn't believe I was supposed to go. Do I have any regrets? Only that I wished I would have danced in at least one show to have experienced what it was like.

Fast forwarding some. In April 2019, I had the privilege of escorting my senior tap dance class from Light of Life Performing Arts Studio to perform a Spanish tap dance to the song "Basic Instructions Before Leaving Earth" on the stage at Times Square with Project Dance. Cheryl Cutlip, a former Radio City Music Hall Rockette and head of Project Dance, whispered to me as my dancers performed "My Dance." Without realizing the impact of her words, Cheryl said, "You could have come to NYC to dance as a Rockette, but God multiplied your gift of dance through all of these young ladies!" I was on Cloud 9! This brought a sense of fulfillment to what I had always wished for.

*Joe S. McIlhaney, Jr., MD and Freda McKissic Bush, MD, Hooked: New Science On How Casual Sex Is Affecting Our Children, Meet the Brain, (Chicago: Northfield Publishing), Chapter 2

Back to my decision to leave New York. I called my boyfriend from a phone in the bathroom at our hotel room. (Who has a phone in the bathroom?) I told him, "Gary, I am coming home. Let's get married!"

It was a long ride back to Baltimore. Silence held sway for a long time, too. My parents had every right at the time to wish so much more for me. I only believe as hard as that must have been for them, my dance was about to be what God intended it to be.

At the age of 19, one year later, Gary and I were married. The first year of our marriage was disastrous, to put it quite mildly. In the sixth month, I was pregnant. It seemed, at the time, to be the worst thing in the world that could have ever happened to me. Where were the Disney books now? My dream was dashed! My Prince Charming was now only a wishful thought. I didn't think my marriage was going to make it.

3
My "It's All About Me" Dance

At the time, I was teaching dance and I did not want to lose my job as a dance instructor and dancer. If I would lose my physical shape, my career was over! I did not want anything or anyone to interfere with *MY dance* career. How selfish I was! So, what do you think I did? I was intensely concerned about my shape, my future in dance as a dancer and my dance instructor jobs! And not seeing a future in our marriage, I decided to walk into Planned Parenthood to get an abortion. For only $150.00 my worries would be over and no one would have to know.

As I walked into the clinic in Baltimore City, second thoughts began piercing my conscience. I started rethinking what I was doing. I wanted to put the procedure on hold and come back another day. As I shared my apprehensions with the nurse, she told me it was too late to back out! The doctor was waiting. What was I to do?

After signing the paper that spelled out the consequences such as I could potentially not be able to have children in the future or I could even die, I thought to myself, my parents have no clue where I am. What if I would die? What if I could never have children?

I was in a state of shock when they took me into the surgical room. Up to this point I had never thought of the child I was carrying as a baby. I was told it was a fetus; just a mass of tissue. This occurred in the era right before the days of the internet, before we could research vital information conveniently online for ourselves. I knew nothing other than what I was told. I was carrying around just a mass of tissue; I didn't have any other explanation. Since several of my friends had already had at least one abortion, I felt it was my only option. It *must* be okay.

After they gave me the local to numb me and began the procedure, while lying on a cold steel hospital bed, I began to feel the pressure and the pain as if my guts were being ripped out. I looked at the nurse next to me and then I heard the doctor say, "Did we get all of the baby?" *The baby? The baby?* Oh, my God! What did I do? It *WAS* a baby!!! *It was 'MY' baby*!!! I lay there helpless as tears began to flow down my face. I just wanted to die! How could I have done this? What was I thinking?

I remember, etched in my mind, the room in which they placed all the girls who had just had abortions, after the procedure. It was like we were cattle-herded into a stall. We didn't even sit on chairs. We all sat on the floor looking around at each other. I was taken aback after I realized a girl in the room was a former classmate. Would she tell anyone? What was SHE doing here? It was embarrassing sitting there with no privacy to cry, grieve or say a word. You could have heard a pin drop. There were no cell phones back then, so we all avoided eye contact. An intimidating silence swayed loudly within the room, no one having the energy to break its oppression.

When I arrived home, I crawled into bed and curled into a ball, in a fetal position, already regretting a decision I could not change. How could I go forward from here and live with myself?

And, never do we think the decisions we make will affect anyone but us. That is just an absolutely vicious lie from the devil! My abortion was the greatest mistake (sin) of my life! One I can never take back. What Satan meant for evil, though, I would eventually allow God to turn it around and make something good come out of it! This is all a part of *my dance*; the good, the bad and the ugly!

My husband knew we were expecting, but I didn't even ask for his consent. I was married. What was I thinking? This was his baby, too. I didn't make this baby alone. But it was ALL about me! So, I took my dance into my own hands. Our marriage was so broken at the time that even though Gary knew what I considered doing, his response was... passivity. Consequently, his detachment affected my decision and I snuffed out the life of our first child.

As a result of 'one' decision, my life was forever changed – not mine alone, but all those around me, then and now! This would be a lifelong regret that dogged me when I least expected it. To my delight I was able to get pregnant five times. After the abortion, the excitement of conceiving was sheer bliss. But the daunting thoughts and disturbing tucked-away images would always rear their ugly heads and remind me of what I did. It was torture when it should have been a joy! I am beyond jubilation at the grace of God in blessing me with three wonderful children and two in Heaven. Not something I deserved – but because of God's loving mercy!

There is a principle in the Bible called sowing and reaping. The decisions we make every day will sow into our lives either good or evil.

"Do not be deceived, God is not mocked; for whatever a man sows, that he will also reap." (Galatians 6:7-9)

4
My Dance of Pain, Forgiveness, and Healing

Growing up with a "goody-two-shoes" image, I could do no wrong in my parent's eyes. I always tried to maintain that image through school, on the honor roll, dancing, as a dance instructor as well as in my community and most of all, with my family. I never wanted to shatter that image. The guilt of knowing I had aborted their first grandchild ate away at me. Several years later after becoming a Christian, it took everything I had within me to approach my parents with what I'd done, but my heart compelled me to sit down with them, as well as my grandmother, to confess to them. I believed they had a right to know. And, I needed to ask them to forgive me. My parents and grandmother were very gracious and kind to me. I think they knew the internal pain I harbored and they wanted to console me. They granted me forgiveness, which lifted my heart. And there was a sense of freedom that happened for me when, instead of safeguarding this secret and keeping it in the darkness, I exposed it into the light. The expulsion out of the darkness and into the light resulted in its loss of intense power over me. Confession of the truth does indeed set us free! And, Gary was about to experience this, too, in time!

When I have gone into the public schools teaching abstinence and have shared my personal story with students, they ask the question, are you still with that guy? I replied, "Well, yes, I am." And we are now celebrating 45 years of marriage.

Many years had now passed and latent issues from the early-on, painful season in our marriage, which never had closure, surfaced. As a result of attending a "Pastor's Intensive" in 1995, our hearts and minds were now sensitive and receptive to asking each other's forgiveness for the pain caused by the abortion. Gary's pain was different than mine. He dealt with the fact that his detachment during that time helped facilitate my carrying through with aborting our first child.

During the "Pastor's Intensive," Gary and I volunteered to take part in a family snapshot where we assigned people from our group to represent each member of our family in what was called a 'human visual.' Members from our group stood in the place of our children; Nicole, Matthew and Joshua. We were then asked if anyone else needed to be included in our family portrait. I spoke up and said, "We had a miscarriage. (I'll share more about that in a little while.) That baby should be in the picture."

Then, my questioning gaze slowly met with Gary's eyes and the unspoken message of resistance from his eyes said - *No. No, I don't want anyone here to know about the abortion.* But, within moments and with heartache, Gary broke down and disclosed, "We also have another child that we aborted."

We then proceeded to add one more person into our family snapshot to represent our aborted child. This made us a family of seven. Our pain and struggle were so palpable in the room that it resulted in not a dry eye in the group. From that day forward, Gary walked through his own healing process. God is now using Gary to help other men understand the pain and their role in this troubling and life-altering decision.

God has used my heartbreak and testimony to spare other babies their death sentence. I know of at least two children who were born after their moms changed their minds. My dance is a dance that will relate to and reach those who have traveled the same road I have, including those family members and friends who have also been deeply troubled by virtue of relationship. I also hope it will help others to avoid making the same mistakes in the first place.

In 1982, God blessed us with Nicole our first and only daughter. What a joy and privilege to have such a beautiful child. Several years later we were trying for a boy. Gary wanted a son to hunt with one day! Well, I got pregnant two years later and the pregnancy seemed to be going well. I was able to continue teaching dance and didn't seem to be picking up weight and was not as nauseated as I was with my pregnancy with Nicole (six months of morning sickness - or should I say 'all the time vomiting' was enough for one pregnancy). Maybe this one was a boy?

A couple weeks into the pregnancy, with a sinking feeling, I went for my checkup because I was spotting blood. The doctor very attentively listened for the baby's heartbeat, but could not detect one. He related to me that since there was no heartbeat evident, I might miscarry. I sat there. Limped and shocked. How could this be? I had been feeling great and everything seemed to be fine.

I went home that day and lost my third child, this time, by miscarriage. Because the doctor did not know if I passed everything, he recommended a Dilation and Curettage (D & C) at the hospital. Gary, my mom and I traveled to Sinai Hospital and the doctor offered me three options. I could stay overnight if I had anesthesia, or have a local needle to numb me from the pain and be there several hours, or no anesthesia and go home as soon as the procedure was over. I chose no anesthesia and no local so I could get the procedure completed and get home to Nicole as soon as possible. Well, never let a male doctor tell you that a D & C is not intensely painful. During the procedure, I gripped my husband's hand so tightly I almost drew blood. The pain was not just physical, but it brought back memories of the first D & C - the abortion. I just wanted to get home and see Nicole and begin recovery.

A couple of months later, in 1984, after grieving the loss of my child through miscarriage, I was tortured with the thought that, because I took the life of my first child, God was making me pay and required taking the life of my third child. This thought heavily haunted me. I know, now, God absolutely does not work that way! *But this awful and agonizing situation* was what God 'turned around,' using it for good as a tool, as I allowed it to draw me to Him! "God is good all the time; all the time God is good!" As a result, pain in my dance was about to change my marriage, my family, my life.

"And we know that ALL things work together for good to those who love God and are called according to HIS purpose." (Romans 8:28)

One year later, in 1985, after seven years of marriage, I left my husband for a couple days and took our daughter Nicole with me. I told Gary I couldn't stay in the marriage unless things changed. In my mind, our options were to either see a counselor or go to church. Gary told me he would go to church.

At the time, Gary was Catholic and it was huge for him to agree to go to a protestant church. Gary consulted with a priest, asking his counsel on what to do about our marriage falling apart and his personal feelings of hopelessness? The priest simply counseled him to be a good husband and father and things will work out. Gary told him he was doing that and it wasn't working. He left the church feeling empty with no direction.

Two Sundays later, I had to arrange delivery of Home Interior products to my grandmother's home after hosting a party, since many relatives purchased home items. In the event that you are not familiar with Home Interior, they manufactured a line of pictures, sconces, candles, and wall hangings in the 1980's; decorations for home or business. My grandmother's home was the place where my mother's eight siblings and spouses would congregate on Sundays to eat breakfast before church or come to lunch after church. So, this was the best and most economical way to deliver everyone's purchases. A one-stop shop!

On Palm Sunday, 1985, I actually decided to attend church and, after the service, take the box of Home Interior items to Gran's (Madeline Carter) house. This was the first time I had visited the Fort Howard Community Church since I was a little girl in Mrs. Cook's Sunday School class. Gary was scheduled to work in the steel mill that Sunday so he couldn't go with Nicole and me. I was intrigued with what the pastor was sharing and told Gary we needed to attend Easter service the following week. At that Sunday worship service, I filled out a visitor's card and requested a pastoral visit. A few days later the pastor called and we set up a meeting.

I was naturally nervous, since I did not know what he would want to talk about, but I knew we needed help in our marriage. Gary expected just a visit from the pastor. But when the peep-hole revealed Pastor Steve Hartland and elder, Harry Iman, were at the door, he turned to me and said, "Oh, great! There are two of them!" Gary had been a little suspicious that whole day, because he was thinking maybe they were going to solicit money. (This may have come from his prior religious upbringing.) He was pleasantly surprised that they never brought up the topic of money all evening. They just wanted to get to know us.

Eventually, the conversation took a turn when the Gospel was shared with me. This was the first time anyone had ever asked me, "Cheryl, if you were to die today, where do you think you would go?" I thought to myself, *well, I think I am a fairly good person. I try to do good things,* but then in the recesses of my conscience, just barely concealed, lodged in there - the abortion. As that truth wiggled its way up to the surface, I was arrested with the real possibility, *Wow! Maybe I'm not as good as I thought?*

I timidly admitted to the pastor I wasn't sure where I would go. He told me that I could know beyond a shadow of a doubt where I would spend eternity. He shared with me the plan that God revealed to the world; a plan He has made available to everyone. Because I was a sinner, the only way to have my sins paid for and eradicated completely was through Jesus Christ, God's Son. He related that Jesus died for me and by placing my trust in Him alone for salvation I would be guaranteed a place in Heaven.

*"Jesus said to him, I am the Way, the Truth and the Life. No one comes to
Father except through Me." (John 14:6)*

It almost seemed too easy to believe and too good to be true. How could I have all my past, present and even future sins completely washed away as if they had never happened? Well, it might have seemed too easy to believe at that moment, but as I started to grasp the severe cost Christ paid, I began to realize what Jesus did for me on a very cruel cross.

Amidst the millions of people on Earth in April 1985, God focused His loving gaze on a 26-year-old woman, reached down to me that night in the living room of our rowhome with His unconditional love and acceptance, and I couldn't help but respond by placing my trust in Christ. My *dance* was now *forever* changed!

"GOD'S GREAT DANCE FLOOR"
Martin Smith, Nick Herbert, Chris Tomlin

I'm coming back to the start where You found me
I'm coming back to Your heart
Now I surrender; take me, this is all I can bring

I'm coming back to the start; I got this freedom
In here we feel Your heart
Your heartbeat for us; take me, this is all I can bring

You'll never stop loving us, no matter how far we run
You'll never give up on us,
All of Heaven shouts: Let the future begin, Let the future begin
Take me; This is all I can bring

I feel alive, I come alive, I am alive on God's great dance floor
I feel alive, I come alive, I am alive on God's great dance floor
God's great dance floor

5

Phil Keaggy

&

Gary's Divine Dance

Now Gary was with me that night I put my trust in Jesus. He was not ready to make the decision, but courteously prayed along with the pastor and did not trust Christ as I did. God was still in the process of drawing Gary to Himself.

Two weeks later, Gary went turkey hunting at his sister's (Cindy) home in the mountains of Knoxville, Maryland, near Harper's Ferry, West Virginia. Gary had all intentions of going, but *not* coming home. He had planned to take his life in the woods while at his sister, Cindy's, where we all would be able to find him. *But... God!* He aimed the shotgun at himself, but was suddenly distracted when he heard a turkey gobble in the distance. God got his attention. After hearing the turkey's gobble, the twelve-gauge shotgun he had turned on himself he, instead, turned the shotgun away toward the turkey. *God can use anything or anyone he wants!* Gary was so excited when he shot the turkey! He forgot all about his troubles for a short time.

After Gary arrived back at his sister's house, she handed him a cassette tape (Remember them?) of Phil Keaggy, the all-time best nine-fingered Christian guitarist. Cindy said, "Gary, listen to this on the way home." With two hours of black asphalt lying ahead, Gary started the engine as he jumped inside the truck, thoroughly thrilled about his conquered catch. The speakers were blasting the airwaves of 98 ROCK. He popped the cassette into the player and began listening to the music.

Cindy had received Christ into her life a year or two before and Gary knew she had become a Christian. The music was actually pleasant to listen to. He pondered. *God has music, too?* As the lyrics of "I Belong to You" landed and implanted into Gary's heart, he felt so emotionally moved... that God was directly speaking to him through the song.

Gary steered the truck to the shoulder of the road, which now for a short time had become an altar of the Lord where the Holy Spirit had settled, and as best he knew how, he cried out to God to save him! At that moment, a former night-club bouncer and body builder was a broken man.

Ten years after the night Gary became a Christian, God blessed him with a divine appointment to speak to Phil Keaggy on a nationwide radio program. The call-in program was speaking with the last caller and Gary had just enough time to tell Phil what God did through his song "I Belong to You." Phil revealed that the song was actually written for his wife. How strange that a song written for one totally different intended purpose was commutated by God to become a saving tool for Gary!

Gary was twenty-eight when our marriage began to change. God rescued a damaged, collapsing marriage, re-sculpted it and made it new! The Lord blessed me with a new beginning. My *dance* was about to change... again! *Our* 'marriage dance' was now changed forever!

Fast-forwarding to 2013. I was listening to our local Christian radio station, WJTL, in York, Pennsylvania, on 'Winning Wednesday.' My ears perked-up and I was momentarily suspended upon hearing the announcer say, "When you hear a Phil Keaggy song, be the first person to call in and you will win two tickets to attend this week's Keaggy concert at The Junction Center." I immediately prayed, "Lord, You know I want to win these tickets for Gary to meet Phil."

Very attentively, I waited and listened so I could respond in warp-speed when I recognized the Keaggy song. I programmed my cell phone to speed dial the radio station at my command. All I needed to hear were three notes of Keaggy's unique style; just three notes. THERE IT WAS! I instantly hit my phone's button. The person who answered my call was stunned that someone called in so fast, since not even one word had yet been sung. I was ecstatic! I shared briefly that I was praying to win these tickets and why. I wanted to treat Gary to Phil's concert in hopes that Gary would have the opportunity to meet Phil and share, in person, how God used Phil's song "I Belong to You" many years ago as the vehicle that turned Gary to Christ. Those tickets included a luncheon meal and a photo with Phil.

That Friday, we arrived at The Junction Center steeped in anticipation of meeting Phil. We were third in line after entering the building and I wasted no time proactively scoping out the best seat for us. The coffeehouse-like atmosphere with small round tables that seated four made a very comfy setting. Pizza and coffee were served. As I was just about to eat my dessert pizza, my eyes caught Phil Keaggy as he turned the corner and approached the room. My heart could have taught Mexican Jumping Beans a new dance! Phil was making his way onto the stage. We were seated in the front row to his right.

When the "on-the-radio" concert began, we were told that Phil would perform his musical selections and would have to leave shortly thereafter. Gary and I looked at each other with a little disappointment, thinking perhaps Gary wouldn't be able to talk to Phil after all. I just sat there and silently prayed, God, we have come so far and we are so close. Please let it be that Gary can share his testimony with Phil.

As Phil began his concert, we were all in awe! Gary leaned over to me and said, "You are witnessing a legend, the greatest guitarist; you have no idea how great he is!" After 30 minutes of humor, humility and raw God-gifted talent flooded our souls, I wondered if Phil would open the floor for song requests. There aren't words to express the depth of delight that overtook us when Phil turned to the crowd and asked if there were any favorites. Not to be denied this once-in-a-lifetime opportunity, I immediately and swiftly propelled my hand into the air, flagged Phil's attention in our direction and called out loudly, "I Belong to You." Phil looked at us and asked, "Is it your anniversary?" Remember, Phil had written this song for his wife. Gary spoke up with a quiver in his voice and said, "Phil, I have been waiting 28 years, 1 month and 5 days to tell you in person that I had planned to take my life one day while on a hunting trip at my sister's home. But after certain circumstances happened and I shot a turkey, I decided to return home. My sister gave me one of your cassettes to listen to on the drive back. After listening to your song, "I Belong to You," I came to know the Lord on the side of a road in Harper's Ferry, West Virginia. I trusted in the Lord in 1985 and have been serving the Lord as a pastor for almost 23 years." The room was filled with teary eyes and sniffles and a tear even trickled down Phil's cheek. He winked at Gary and began the song. What a day of wonder! God's providential timing! By the way, this was one of two things on Gary's 'bucket list,' which God has answered. Again, God granted us a desire of our hearts. God is so good!

> *"You have turned my mourning into dancing; You have put off my sackcloth and clothed me with gladness, to the end that my glory may sing praise to You and not be silent. O, LORD my God, I will give thanks to You forever."*
> *(Psalm 30:11-12)*

"I BELONG TO YOU"
Music & Lyrics by Phil Keaggy

I belong to you, and you're coming into view,
My heart revived when you arrived to make it all come true.
With each drop of rain and like the morning dew,
Like the wind I whisper your sweet name, Oh I belong to you.

I cannot be sad when I think of times we've had.
My memory brings near to me Your voice and I am glad.
All the world's on stage waiting for their cues,
All my lines you're free to rearrange, 'cause I belong to you.
Holding your hand, I will go where you may lead,
You've got the right to speak your words of love to me.
And I understand that you've never done me wrong.
I'm right where I belong here with you.

I belong to you, and I love the things you do
The things you say in every way, your tenderness comes through.
When my work is done and my life's in review,
Oh to hear these words spoken to me, child I belong to you

6
Dance Lessons of Life

"It's a Wonderful Life" is not just an endearing, nostalgic movie our family has watched annually at Christmas, but I can emphatically say that I relished my childhood living and breathing a real *wonderful life*. An icon from my early years was the great Shirley Temple. Every Sunday morning, I would be glued to the black and white TV screen to watch her perform a song and tap dance. I loved the clickety-clack of those tap shoes - I needed me some.

Dance was everything to me from the time I entered that dance studio at age three. As I mentioned previously, I will be forever grateful for the tremendous financial sacrifices my parents made to facilitate the pursuit of my passion to dance. They did whatever it took for me to have all the accessories I needed - tap and ballet shoes, costumes, ballet attire, pointe shoes, and even a fake cascade hairpiece to look like other girls with long hair and more!

Performing for my parents became a daily occurrence. My first remembrance of this was to the endearing children's song, "I'm a Little Teapot" written by George Harold Sanders and Clarence Z. Kelley, published in 1939.

> I'm a little teapot, short and stout
> Here is my handle, here is my spout
> When I get all steamed up, hear me shout
> Tip me over and pour me out!

Someone, please tell me you remember this song! All pretty in pink and decked out with ballet shoes, tights and a pale pink leotard, dress-ups and costumes became my second wardrobe in my very special second world.

A highlight of my youth of epic proportion occurred when I was hand-selected by the elementary teachers for a reindeer solo in the Christmas play. Several months later, I was specifically selected to perform the Sugar Plum Fairy pointe solo. What elation overcame me!

On my opening night with my family and grandmothers in attendance, two dance numbers prior to my debut, a persistent screeching alarm sounded in the distance. Everyone started running backstage as all chaos erupted. I was 11 years old at the time and I was in a scurry trying to understand what "evacuate the building" meant. Apparently, the police department received a phone call that a bomb had been planted inside the building. Why now? Why me – on my first-ever solo? On a lighter note, I initially thought they were saying "Vacuum the building." I couldn't understand why. The bomb-scare just rearranged a special highlight in my dance. The good news is that the next night I was able to perform the Sugar Plum solo!

Dance Masters of America training classes employed stellar dance teachers across America. At age 11, being trained and mentored by the topmost dance teachers in the U.S. was bigger than life for someone so young! When I was pulled on stage with my idol Gus Giordano* to do a jazz dance to "Green Onions," out of hundreds of young girls, I knew he must have recognized something special in me. Wow! This was only one of my special memories of the Dance Masters Conventions.

Time Out!

My dad was full boar into softball. He developed the Dundalk, Maryland, softball program from ground zero and then expanded it into other leagues and areas. I grew up around roster sheets, ball players at the house, games almost every night of the week, tournaments on the weekends and traveling places with the team to Championships! I even became the official Bat Girl of the team with a hat, baseball pants, jersey and uniform. I just wanted to spend time with my dad no matter what that looked like. I am so proud that years later, my dad was inducted into the Greater Dundalk Sports Hall of Fame and Maryland Slow-Pitch Hall of Fame. He also had the honor of a softball field named after him in Merritt Park in Dundalk.

As a young girl wanting to please her dad, I decided one year to enroll in the girls' softball program in the local recreation council. I thought perhaps because I was coordinated in dance that I could naturally play softball. Consequently, dad and I spent time together greasing the baseball glove with Vaseline, wrapping it with rubber bands, and dad teaching me to catch, throw and hit the ball. But when the time came to start on the team, my nerves got the best of me (or should I say the worst of me). Our team, "The Warriors," was scheduled for our first game and my proud family was there rooting me on! Sitting on the bench knowing that within a couple more players I would be up at bat, it felt like thousands of butterflies were fluttering everywhere in my stomach. I really needed to hit the bathroom. But – no bathrooms at the field! Oh, no! I told my coach I needed to go and she advised me to find the closest house in the neighborhood and ask if I could use their bathroom. So, I ran to the rowhomes next to the field and someone was so kind to let me use theirs. That wasn't the only time I had to escape to go to the bathroom before my turn at bat. It became a regular occurrence. I was smitten with fear to bat or even play in the game. As a result, I sat on the bench the entire season. At the Softball Awards Ceremony, I was shocked to hear my name called. I received my "Baltimore Recreation Award for Participation and Achievement in Softball" certificate in December 1969, for trying at softball. My parents and I knew then that I should stick with dancing!

*Gus Giordano (July 10, 1923 – March 9, 2008) - American jazz dancer; founder of Giordano Jazz Dance Chicago; performed both on and off Broadway as well as many other platforms for the arts, a brilliant choreographer, wrote the Anthology of American Jazz Dance, an expert instructor, he actualized the Jazz Dance World Congress. He will always be recognized as an important and respected force in the founding of jazz dance.

The Lord endowed me with a talent I could excel in, even though it was not always easy. My body shape is tall and bigger-boned. This may have come from my German family background. My husband says we are built like "Panzers" (a German tank). I also have flat feet, which forced me to work extra hard forming an arch for pointing my feet.

By the time I was 12, I was performing in Atlantic City, New Jersey. This was before the days of the casinos and gambling. Atlantic City was a fun beach and boardwalk vacation destination for families. I can still smell the roasted peanuts at the Planter's Peanut Store. I remember the Diving Show where a girl mounted a horse high above the crowd and dove into a pool of water below, the underwater adventure ride in a small submerged vessel and the waffles with strawberries and whipped cream! Yum!

It was the home of the Tony Grant Stars of Tomorrow on the Steel Pier. Our dance studio would travel and perform with other young talents: ventriloquist acts, singers, jugglers and dancers. The closest show today to identify with would be the TV show, "America's Got Talent." The highlight of my summers was the adventure of a road trip tour with my girlfriends and their families–three years in a row!

Back home, dressed up in my black hot-pants and halter-top sporting white, stretched, knee-high boots, I was asked to be a "Go-Go Dancer" in the Woody Allen play, "Play It Again, Sam" at the Spotlight Theater in downtown Baltimore, Maryland. Though I was only 13 at that time, I looked like a 21-year-old in the play. In a small basement theater-in-the-round (it is actually square-designed to always assure a clear shot of the stage and actors to the audience) I had my big line to say: "Get lost, creep." You will never know how many times I practiced those three words. This was my first and only experience in acting. I was better at dancing!

At 14 years old, I was also accepted to the Baltimore Ballet Theater under the direction of Wally Saunders in Reisterstown, Maryland. Wally was renowned for having the Hollywood actress, Goldie Hawn (raised in Takoma Park, MD), as a dance student. A favorite memory was when we were performing at the Lyric Theater in Baltimore City. I remember having low self-esteem at the time because the dancers were all so pretty, talented and had flowing long hair that was woven into a beautiful ballet bun. My hair was short and looked far different. I placed a fake bun on the back of my head, loaded with endless bobby-pins, to prevent the embarrassment of my hairpiece falling off while performing! My female dance teacher at the time knew my insecurity and took my face into her hands and told me I was beautiful. She believed in me... so, I danced!!!

At 14 and 15, opportunities opened to dance at the City Fair in Baltimore with big guns such as Benny Goodman, the King of Swing; Joe Williams; Buddy Rich and Zim Zemarel. In case you are too young to know these names, these are men who built the 'Swing Era' and Big Band songs like "Sing, Sing, Sing," "Stompin' at the Savoy" and "One O'Clock Jump."

I was also privileged to travel with George Goebel, a native Baltimore, Maryland, magician, who was the 'first' magician to incorporate dancers into his magic show. Our dance class performed with Mr. George at many local functions in Maryland and we were also invited to participate at a Magician's Convention in Indiana.

One Magic Revue show in Frederick, Maryland, was a show that none of us will ever forget! The "Tyahama Torture Harness" was a trick that included a restraining device and harness, which strapped belts around Mr. George restricting his arms and shoulders, a buckle between his legs and cuffing his hands behind his back.

The scene opens with a harness held high and an invitation to an audience participant to come up onto the stage, inspect the torture device to make sure it is sturdy and then tighten the device on Mr. George. We had seen this act so many times that we didn't flinch at it, because Mr. George was easily able to get out of the harness without a glitch every time.

This particular show, Mr. George happened to call my fiancé, Gary, up onto the stage to check the apparatus and tighten the straps before he would signal his assistant to raise the curtain and start the music while he wiggles out of the harness. During our dating days, Gary was working out and bodybuilding; quite the buff guy. He was asked to inspect the harness and make sure it was solid, and then asked to securely fasten the buckles and chains and pull them tight. Once he finished, Mr. George always asked the question, "Is that the best you can do?" Gary looked at the buckles and put his hip into the side of Mr. George and proceeded to pull the straps two notches beyond their appropriate place not knowing, at the time, that the deep grooves in the well-worn belt were where the buckles needed to be located in order for all to run smoothly with the timing of the music. The look on Mr. George's face said it all. He had never had anyone tighten the harness to the place where it would break his ribs.

Mr. George directed his assistant to hand Gary a watch to calculate the time as his two assistants raised the small curtain in order to hide his body. As the clock began to tick away, I could hear all the girls behind stage talking and some were crying. I was part of this performance, so I was in costume for the next magic act. I asked the girls what was wrong. They replied that Gary had taken the belt too far for Mr. George to get out of the harness and the song kept playing over and over. As Gary counted off the seconds that grew into minutes, now I began to cry. I knew he had no idea what he had done and seeing the pain in Mr. George's face made me cringe. He would normally be out of the harness in twelve seconds flat and the assistants would drop the curtain. As he began to contort every muscle within to escape the harness, he was finally released! Somehow, he found a method to get out that he had never used before. The audience's deafening silence erupted into a roaring applause. It all ended well and the show went on, but we were never the same again when this trick was performed at each show.

Many years later I heard that Mr. George had actually broken several ribs during that performance, but being the man he was, he never complained.

On the Fourth of July in Dundalk, where I grew up, the town always gathers for a celebration with a parade: The Heritage Fair and the Miss Independence Competition. Well, here I go again. I couldn't pass up the opportunity to dance once again on stage. The tap dance to "I've Got Rhythm" was my competition highlight. Participation in that contest awarded me the honor of first runner-up. Riding in the parade on the back of a convertible along with the winner and the 2nd runner-up, perfecting my princess wave as we made our way past the crowd, was the highlight of my day. But could it get any better? It sure did! I was privileged to meet the famed football quarterback, Johnny Unitas of the Baltimore Colts on the Grandstand. Oh, what a day!

During high school graduation year, the class selected me as the Senior Class Superlative's Best Female Dancer of the Patapsco Class of 1977.

At 20, I had the privilege of leading our dance troupe at the Baltimore City Civic Center for the renowned and distinguished Hollywood entertainer, Bob Hope. My first Hollywood star encounter! I will share more about this in another chapter.

So, you can see. I had an extraordinary childhood with many dreams fulfilled and opportunities way beyond what I could have ever imagined. I share all of these things for you to understand *my life-dance* and the Dance Lessons God prepared for me.

Moving forward again, when I became a born-again Christian in April 1985, a tug-of-war began in my heart. I struggled with the idea of teaching dance steps and moves that I thought were cute, but were also inappropriately sensual and sexual for young girls to perform. After teaching dance since I was 15, when I turned 26, I believed God was calling me out of all I ever knew; all that I trained for in life. But this was what I did best! It was all I knew how to do!

When I would leave my three-year old daughter, Nicole, to go teach dance, while on the drive to the studio, I would cry. What was this? What was happening? I couldn't understand why something I loved so passionately was now producing conflicting feelings and felt like it was being extracted out of me. I longed to be a stay-at-home mom like my mom was for me. I agonized, prayed and cried; I could not understand why I did not want to go back to dance or even teach dance. I also did not understand that God was tweaking the gift He had given me.

The following year as I began the fall semester at the studio, I found out that I was pregnant and due in June. So, I taught tap until June and then delivered Matthew (Gift of God) Ryan, our firstborn son. God had now blessed me with two children! Thank the Lord I was able to bear children. There are women, who, after having an abortion, are not able to have children.

I have been speaking and sharing with women and young girls about my abortion since I gave my life to Christ. Over those years, several women have approached me in tears because their abortion stole from them the ability to bear a child. No woman can say with utmost assurance: *Oh, that will never happen to me.* I don't know what I would have done if I could not have given birth to my own children as a result of my own selfish actions. God's loving-kindness has overwhelmed me!

After Matthew was born, God made it clear to me it was time to stop teaching dance. I thought my world was coming to an end! It was my world as I loved and knew it. Why was God targeting *my* dance? What would I *do* now? He wasn't saying anything to my husband about his hunting -- ha-ha! When we married, I think we included 'in dancing or hunting' during our vows along with "for better or worse, for richer or poorer, in sickness and in health!"

Four years following Matthew's birth, God blessed us with another son, Joshua (God is my Salvation) Michael. Our family was complete. The Lord blessed us with three beautiful children. The greatest tools God has used to humble me, teach me and encourage me in my walk with the Lord have been my children.

Nicole has always made me laugh with her crazy sense of humor and 'best friend' connection. She is a strong woman with courage, determination and great conviction. Being her Matron of Honor in her wedding was a culmination of our relationship and such a privilege! We are now mother, daughter and *friends*.

Matthew, with his quick wit and funny sayings, has always made my heart smile. Matthew has accomplished so much for such a young man, from being the first named inventor of a Patent, traveling across the globe for business development, President of two entities, and serving as a Board Member on the Archery Trade Association.

Joshua, being the baby of the family, is more relaxed than all of us combined. He has so many gifts and talents. Josh has toured the country with several bands and has landed in LA, California. His creativity always amazes me - from videography to his musical ability. He, too, has that keen sense of humor that catches me off-guard and makes me laugh.

Our kids did not get their 'wit or comical inclinations' from me. That is their father's gift. I've been told that I'm more serious than all my kids combined. So, God knew He would use my husband and children in my life to show me how to 'lighten up and live!'

The Dance Lessons of Life continue through all seasons of life! I was entering a new chapter of my Dance and another new season of life.

7
Dancing with the Stars

My mom thoroughly enjoyed the evenings when she was able to settle down to watch television and view "Dancing with The Stars." This is a program where they invite people like comedians, singers, actors, athletes and others who have had little to no dance background to participate with a partner in several categories of ballroom dancing like: the jitterbug, quick step, samba, waltz, etc. Each weekly segment presents a challenge of new steps and dances to perform. At the season finale, the dancing team with the most votes wins the trophy. My experience of dancing with a Hollywood star involves the story of legendary comedian, Bob Hope.

Bob Hope. I wonder how many people will know his name. If you are a baby boomer like me, Bob Hope was a household name growing up in the 60's, 70's and 80's! My 'famous dance' was when I was selected by my dance instructor, Jean Kettell, to lead our dance troupe at the Baltimore Civic Center in Maryland for the Preakness Opening Show in May 1979. Mr. Hope's favorite song to introduce him to a crowd before he would woo them with stand-up comedy for about an hour was "Thanks for the Memories." Our dance studio was selected to perform a tap dance to this trademark song as we would prep the crowd for the gala event. Bob Hope was a British-born, naturalized American citizen (1920), comedian and actor who appeared in vaudeville, on Broadway and in radio, television and movies. He was also noted for his work with the US Armed Forces and his numerous USO shows entertaining American military personnel throughout his long career. He was fittingly honored for his humanitarian work. Bob Hope appeared in or hosted approximately 60 USO shows in his lifetime. His purpose was to bring our troops a little bit of home and the USA while they were abroad. What an honor for our girls to be selected and a greater honor for me to be hand-picked as the leader to oversee them!

Walking into the Baltimore Civic Center (today the Mariner Arena) was a humbling experience. It seemed so big! The stage WAS so big! The crowd attending was so big! This was a really *big* deal! This was unequivocally the biggest event in my dance career!

On the night of the performance, the dancers wondered if we would actually get to see this legend of a man. Could we get an autograph? Bob Hope made us all relax with his invitation to his dressing room. How can 20 girls fit into one man's changing room? Believe me; we made a way! At the age of 76, it was a highlight for him and for us! He had a way of calming us all down with a joke or two and made us feel like we had always been his friends! So, when we lined up backstage for our entrance, we were now connected to the man we would be introducing.

Lights, camera, action! This was the grandest stage I had ever danced upon. To say I had the jitters would be an understatement. As I emerged onto the stage with our entrance combination, our first steps gliding across the platform, I was struck with the brightest lights I had ever encountered. So bright, I couldn't see anyone in the audience. That was perfectly okay, too! Our rhinestone-studded, black, shiny costumes sparkled like stars! And, stars we were - for one night! I was in my glory as I tapped across the stage doing what I was born to do my entire life -- tap dance!

After we danced off the stage, Bob Hope casually strolled onto the stage as the crowd stood with thunderous applause. He appeared calm, casual, and as comfortable as an old shoe. Our time with Mr. Hope made an indelible, awe-inspiring impression on all the dancers.

Many years later, 2003, we learned Bob Hope had passed away at the ripe old age of 100; it was a sad day. Not only was he special to me, but to all the countless lives he touched throughout the dance of his life. I am one that will never forget my encounter with him, all because of "Dancing with the Stars!"

So many people never experience a star opportunity, but all have the ability to dance. For me, I'm not coordinated at hip-hop, even though I love trying. There are different strokes for different folks. I know what I am good at and I try to stick with that. If I attempt to do Irish tap, I'm out of my league. You may have someone who can perform lyrical or contemporary dance, but not be able to tap a step in time. I'm impressed with people who can do just about any type of dance, like the young dancers in the show "So You Think You Can Dance." You have to be so well coordinated and trained. It truly is a gift!

It is funny how, as tiny children, we learn to bounce and twirl to the beat and rhythm of music. We naturally 'feel' the rhythm. Ruth Bell Graham once said, "When Jesus put the little child in the midst of His disciples, He did not tell the little child to become like His disciples; He told the disciples to become like the little child." We need to see life through the eyes of a child – sparkling, fun, playful, carefree, trusting and free to dance! Even if we think we cannot dance – everyone can dance – even though some are better than others. But we can all dance!

Webster's definition of dance is "an emotional move of the body; to move rhythmically." We very rarely think of emotions playing out as a part of dance. Think about it though. When you watch a performance of the Nutcracker and the prima-ballerina has exhausted every ounce of energy, muscles and her body, she has portrayed the epitome of emotions. Her enthralling dance captivates the audience, awarding them with a riveting experience.

Our dance in real life is all about God, not about us, even though our world tells us the opposite. We are taught that we should do what we want, when we want and the way we want. Dance has been redefined and continues to be redefined into new expressions; some not so good. As a result, some of us are afraid to dance. Maybe you grew up in a home where you weren't able to dance due to religious convictions. Maybe you were told 'dancing' is bad; it is of the world and we should have nothing to do with it. Maybe your idea of God doesn't allow you to look outside the box you placed yourself in or someone else placed you in. But for me, I grew up dancing and having the freedom to express myself through many forms of dance. There is nothing like the ability to express oneself through the art of dancing to music. So, to me, when I became a Christian, I did not have any convictions against dance.

After much time in prayer and meditating on the Bible, God led me to give up what was closest to my heart, my love for dance; not because it was wrong, but I needed to grow further in Christ. Seventeen years later God gave me back the gift of teaching dance. At the Light of Life Performing Arts studio, I have the freedom to teach tap and share Christ with my students through prayer and life circumstances; with girls, boys, and women of all ages. I also teach younger ages in the ballet/tap program at the local Jewish Community Center.

Webster's Definition of Choreography

"The art of arranging a dance performance and the notation of the steps of dance in detail."

Part of my teaching job is to choreograph dances for the end of each season or session of dance. This is a joyous and entertaining opportunity for parents, family and friends to watch with pride their dancer's accomplishments at their shows. Choreography is uniquely an art in itself. The design of dance combined with the patterns of people moving about makes dance come alive before your eyes. The thrill of anticipation saturates me from the birth of creative thoughts to converting them into an actual dance on the stage and watching it performed.

God is the Supreme Choreographer. From eternity past, He knew your life and every step you would take, whether you would choose to walk with God or walk your own path. God has given us the ability to enjoy the movements of music, but in the *dance of life*, He is the Choreographer -- the arranger of the dance performance to even the tiniest details of the *dance*! We are not called to aid Him, help Him or choreograph our own dance. God arranges the very best steps for us and we can't go wrong when we surrender our dance into His hands.

"Trust the LORD with all your heart, and lean not on your own understanding; in all your ways acknowledge Him and He shall direct your paths." (Proverbs 3:5-6)

Our Father is definitely a God of the details from the time you were created in your mother's womb as well as throughout your childhood and beyond. God is the *ultimate arranger* of the details of your life, your family and everyone around you. But you have to allow Him to lead your dance and choreograph it, not resist Him. You are the only one who can perform your dance; no one else can. It is scripted and designed for you alone. So, dance like a Star!

"For I know the plans I have for you," says the LORD. "They are plans for good and not for disaster, to give you a future and a hope." (Jeremiah 29:11)

8
The Sacred Dance

In life we always long for relationships. God created within us the desire to be relational. Some of our friendships may last a lifetime, but most are for a season. Our family has had the privilege of having several families, not related by blood, to journey with us – in addition to our natural family, of course. Our family sacrificed for us when we relocated each time through their blood, sweat and tears! But this section is about those whom God brought into our lives at certain times for His purposes and reasons.

My oldest childhood friend, Joyce Ann, and I have treasured memories riding to dance, eating McDonald's burgers and milkshakes, traveling to New Jersey for dance and we have sustained a lifelong friendship!

I think back to our friends, Tosha and Jim, godparents to our daughter, Nicole. Tosh and I share some humorous memories in dance. She remembers a particular time we performed at the Maryland Waxter Center for a benefit, when we were changing into our costumes behind a curtain, which was very rare to do. A little Asian man opened the curtain and peeked at the girls changing and reacted in an Asian accent, "Oh, Boy!" We still laugh at this today! I remember another time how Tosha rescued me during a pointe dance where we wore graduation robes and had a diploma in our hands. At one point, I accidentally dropped my diploma. When we got to the section where we were to bend forward in a circle, Tosh had picked up my diploma and tried to hand it to me. I thought she was giving me hers so I was reluctant to take it. That is when she said, "TAKE IT, Dummy; it's yours!" Thanks, Tosh, for all our laughs and memories!

During Bible college days, God introduced us to two families who journeyed for five years with us supplying gifts and supplementing Nicole's education in Christian school. The Davidsons and The Corbetts entered our lives supporting us with monthly checks and gifts, being the hand of God by helping supply our needs. We had the most sanctified mailbox in Baltimore! I kept a journal during those days with daily updates as God supplied! I remember one story that taught me in the early days as a Christian that God not only provides our needs, but sometimes the desires of our hearts, too!

Most of the time while Gary was in college, I manned the home front. He would leave our Baltimore home in the early morning and travel approximately an hour to Lanham, Maryland, to work and attend Washington Bible College. He started out his day working as a pressman for the college and then attended classes from 8:00-2:00pm. After classes he returned to the print shop to make a part-time income (this was an income reduction from $48,000 in the early 1980s to $15,000).

Gary would finally arrive home around 6:00 in the evening, eat dinner and then retreat to his desk to complete homework and study. This didn't leave a lot of time for family interaction, but we willingly made the necessary adjustments during his five years of college. I was the mom and dad until the weekend and, even then, we did not see much of each other on Sundays with Sunday School and morning and evening church services. We were soaking in all we could get!

Now, let's get back to the *desire* of my heart. One December, the month of our anniversary, Gary wanted to buy something special for me. I knew we didn't have the money but he was determined. Gary asked me if there was anything I needed. I replied, "I need a watch to be on time to preschool and church events." I had seen a circular from BEST Products in the mail and was looking at watches. I saw a gold band with a black face and a diamond chip in the center. *Boy! If there was only one watch I'd love to adorn my arm, this was it!* I thought to myself. I never told Gary this, nor showed him the circular because I knew we didn't have the money.

A few days later, he came home with a beautifully wrapped box and handed it to me saying, "Happy Anniversary!" I was so surprised and humbled. As I opened the small box, I began to think... *it is a watch.* And, yes, it was! It was the very watch I had dreamed of from that BEST Products circular. My words flew from my tongue at breakneck speed as I said, "How did you know? I never told you. Where did you get it? How did you get the money?" He then explained that he had done a printing job for a friend at the college, but he didn't want to accept any money for the job. The friend told him that was unacceptable and that he wanted to do something special for us. Gary told him I needed a watch, which he couldn't afford to buy. Unbeknownst to Gary, his friend purchased a watch, wrapped it up and said, "Give this to your wife." Gary had never even seen the watch I desired and didn't know what was in the box. In all the excitement, I ran upstairs, scarfed up the circular, sailed back down the stairs and presented the circular to Gary showing him that "*it*" was the precise watch I had wished for. I sat there stunned and so thankful that God knows the desires of our hearts. There are even some dance partners in life whom we never personally meet or get to know. I never knew the man who blessed me with the watch! This unforgettable incident engraved in my mind, as a new Christian, how God cares for the desires of our hearts as well as our needs!

"Delight yourself also in the Lord, And He shall give you the desires of your heart." (Psalm 37:4)

Gary and I served in a wonderful fellowship at Fort Howard Community Church in Fort Howard, Maryland. The church congregation sacrificially gave to our family as we pursued ministry. I had never seen God work in a church as He did through this small group of godly people. They gave meals, money, shoes, clothing, support and more. This church demonstrated to us the love of God by providing for us during Gary's years in Bible College. We were under the leadership of two pastors: Pastor Steve Hartland (who introduced us to a personal relationship with the Lord) and Pastor Charles Jennings. We were blessed by the rich expository teaching which grounded us in a solid Biblical foundation. There were others who partnered in the dance with us who gave and gave and gave! We learned what true fellowship and sacrificial love is in Christ.

It is here where we met our spiritual parents, Frank and Flo (recently went home to Jesus). They have journeyed with us from day one of our spiritual odyssey. They changed our diapers (spiritually speaking), wiped our mouths, fed us and lifted us up when we fell down. Their beach home in the Outer Banks has been a place of refuge for our whole family! We treasure so many memories! The Simanskys have paved the way spiritually for us many times! They have been there throughout all the *dances* we have encountered and sacrificed for us through prayer, tears and endless conversations.

After Gary graduated from Washington Bible College in 1991, we served the Lord in the small nautical town of Cambridge, Maryland, for three years at Faith Community Church. God opened this ministry door just six days before Gary graduated from Bible College. Gary had been a Christian for only six years at this time and this is where we got our ministry-feet wet.

We packed up our family and belongings and headed to the Eastern Shore of Maryland, just an hour and 15 minutes from our Baltimore home. This was a time for our family to reconnect and draw closer after the demands on Gary during the Bible College days. Our home was a parsonage only 12 feet from the church. The Golden Shore Christian School, where Nicole and Matt attended, sat diagonally across the street. Our home, our church and Christian school were a holy triangle. Our world was small, but good.

Though Gary had a great education at Washington Bible College and an internship at Fort Howard Community Church, one can never really understand ministry until actually working in it. We learned the hard way, which usually seems to stick. Some people God brought into this season of the dance are friends with whom we still keep in touch through Christmas cards like Bob and Susan. We have never met a more class act couple in ministry. Their four boys are a light and example to us all; a family who genuinely serves and loves God! Bob was one of the leaders who made a huge impact in Gary's life. He fathered him without even realizing it.

I have some funny stories and memories from Faith Community Church. Here is one that I think will make you laugh as it did us. I have changed names to ensure privacy.

An older couple attended our church. We will call them Wes and Alice. One Sunday when we were celebrating our Thanksgiving service to the Lord, we placed a barren tree on the platform. We provided apple ornaments in a basket that could be placed on the tree symbolizing praise to God for what He had done in one's life over the last year. Wes wanted to be one of the first to come forward and give God praise. He told his story about how he met Alice at the assisted living home. He said he had a dream and in it he saw a naked woman - Alice. Wes said God told him to go and take that woman as his wife! Now at this time our son Matt and his friends, who were all about six years of age, dropped their jaws to the floor. They had never before heard praise like this. Frankly, neither had we. A microphone can be a dangerous device in a church! Gary wanted to rush to the front and snatch the mic out of Wes's hand, but he waited.

Then Wes proceeded to tell how they got married. Well, Wes and Alice were in their 70s and Wes was thrilled to announce that they were now expecting! We all shifted in our seats and looked around at each other puzzled and thought, "Did we hear him correctly? Alice was expecting? How could this be in your 70s?"

After church, the buzz going around the room was louder than the Egyptian plague of locusts in the Bible. No one told Gary how to handle a situation like this in Bible College. I guess they pretty much only prepare a person with the Bible head-knowledge part of ministry? Bible college can't possibly anticipate every potential where the rubber meets the road in a local church or pastoral scenarios. As the weeks and months rolled on, we found out Alice was supposed to be carrying twins. The time came when we should have a shower if this was all true, but no one in our church wanted to participate because they said Alice had formerly had a hysterectomy. Nevertheless, Alice was actually given a shower by some of her friends.

Gary asked, "Is this even possible that she could be pregnant?" She actually was getting bigger! I didn't think it could be so, but we knew sooner or later (definitely later) she would have to produce the babies.

One Sunday morning before church, around the time Alice would be due, Gary answered the phone in the parsonage. I could see the expression on his face. As I overheard his conversation I began to think, "What do we do?" Now according to Wes, Alice had a miscarriage at home (mind you, this was at 9 months). Gary put his hand over the receiver (the headset on the old phones had a big handle with a mouthpiece and earpiece) and asked how that could be possible at 9 months? I looked at him completely perplexed. Then, Wes asked if Gary would share this information with the church. Oh, no! We dreaded the inevitably predictable reaction all morning! After he dropped this prayer request into the congregation's lap with as little details as possible, the noise of the locusts returned! This was part of the ministry dance we were not prepared for, but chuckle over to this day. Perhaps Alice had some unresolved life issues and just wanted so badly to conceive? As I look back, I hope I showed her the love she needed through it all! Just prior to our move from Faith Community Church to Pennsylvania, Alice and Wes came to church and told us that Alice was pregnant again and with twins! Gary was glad we were moving on. I concurred.

So, after three years pastoring at Faith Community Church, we moved to Pennsylvania to pastor a church in a mountainous city; a coal mining town huge in diversity of cultures and religion. It was a melting pot during the depression and was in recovery-mode from the flood of 1992 when Hurricane Agnes affected the coal mines and flooded most of the valley. We resided in the township of Kingston, Pennsylvania, a nice place to raise a family.

Unfortunately, though, we experienced our hardest, most difficult times in ministry in this area church. There were many hurtful incidences that wore heavy on us. We still bear deep scars from what we went through during this part of our sacred dance. I can only say that this part of our dance as a family forced us closer together. We really needed each other because we were all we had -- and God. "That which does not kill us makes us stronger." (Paraphrase by G. Gordon Liddy of the Friedrich Nietzche quote)

In the middle of this peace-challenging season, the silver lining was the friendships of certain people whom God had purposely prepared to surround and fortify us. These friends were the bright spots of that time and played a huge part in helping us to heal from a heap of pain.

God favored us with two amazing families who stuck by us during that tumultuous time. We deeply appreciate our dance partners, the Parry family, who were a healing bandage while we nursed church-related open wounds. Denise continues to be a dear friend and sister who is a long-distance dance partner in life.

Another couple very close in heart, The Duartes, entered our lives and blessed us beyond belief. We enjoyed a little over one short wonderful year of close friendship with the Duarte family in Wilkes-Barre before they relocated to San Angelo, Texas. Our families were blessed with a continued relationship by sharing life together with visits to their Texas home, which included deer hunting. Gary preached at their church and Nicole stayed with them while ministering at House of Faith on a short-term mission trip.

One indelible experience while living in Kingston was the winter when we received a record snowfall and within days the weather dramatically warmed up reducing the snowmen to water, which coursed its way back into the Susquehanna River. The fast-melting snow created a probability for flooding in January of 1996, and brought the communities in the valley, as well as those in surrounding areas, back to the emotional memories of the devastating flood of 1972 from Hurricane Agnes. We knew when we purchased our home, we were in a flood zone, but having never gone through a flood before, we thought... *what were the chances?* Well, here we were sitting in our home glued to the news while they assessed the possibility of how likely the levy would break and flood our area. Due to prior floods, the good news was that precautions had been taken and dikes were built up, in addition to sandbags strategically situated.

It is a little disconcerting when you hear a police car cruising through your street broadcasting by megaphone to evacuate your home as soon as possible. My mind started racing to determine what we could save in our home. This home had already been through one flood; could it take two? The first flood actually split apart the seam of the roof, which was now held together by a metal beam. In a hurry, I grabbed what I didn't want to do without - pictures and important documents. Then, as I proceeded to gather Nicole, Matt, and Josh out of bed, I saw Gary go by me with his guns and ammo. At first, I was thinking, *are you kidding me?* But we laugh about this now! The kids were loaded in the car but we still needed to fetch, Patch, the hamster, and, Nugget, the golden Retriever.

As we began to pull away from the house, I paused and looked back, wondering if we would ever see our home the same again? We drove in two separate cars and had to cross the Market Street Bridge now covered with policemen directing people out of town. The water had risen so high at this point that it was merely a foot from surging over the banks. We watched tree stumps, ice blocks, and appliances surging down the river. Gary decided to speak out in faith like Moses! He stopped on the bridge, got out of the car (I can't believe we weren't scolded by the police), stood at the side of the bridge, lifted his arms and prayed, "In the Name of Jesus, I ask that the waters recede and we will not have a flood!" We waited a minute, but then realized we needed to beat it out of the valley and get up the mountain fast!

We stayed with a family in our church that graciously took us in that night. Through all the excitement we finally fell asleep watching the news late into the morning hours. Kids being kids - they were having fun with our unexpected sleepover with friends. The morning gifted us with inexplicable news and great relief that the flood waters had indeed receded and we were free to return home. It appears Gary's prayer was actually effective! What a testimony to God being so gracious to us and everyone else in the area! We ever thank You, merciful, Heavenly Father.

So, in 1997 when we felt God's call to relocate to York, Pennsylvania, we did not buy a home in the flood zone! We found ourselves transitioning from the majestic mountains to the rural countryside of cattle and farmland as far as the eye could see. From the beginning of our ministry life together, we traversed from the nautical, cobblestone streets, sail boats, sea gulls and water galore in Cambridge, Maryland, to the mountains, valleys and panoramic view in Kingston, Pennsylvania, now to the rural rolling hills of York, Pennsylvania! We were closer to family and nearer to what we call home (Baltimore, Maryland). Actually, we recognize that this life is temporary and we recall... *this is not our home; our true home is in Heaven!* Moving to York was a change for our family and we still reside in the same home, today. This is where the kids will always call home because we have lived here longer than anywhere else.

Gary pastored a small community church in York for eight years. During those years God took us to the woodshed (funny thing - we live on a road named "Woodshead"). In this pastorate, we experienced various heartaches over many church families. With a church membership of 125, having 14 marriages fall apart was devastating. There wasn't time for church growth when the people were sliding into sin like an avalanche. The church was in survival mode for a long time. Gary's installment as pastor followed the previous pastor who had fallen into sin, so we inherited clean-up duty! In 2005, after eight years of hard and draining ministry, Gary resigned. A church in Colorado was urging him to come west. We believed this was where we were going next -- Parker, Colorado. Colorado Rockies, here we come!

I was certainly ready for change; maybe the West was our next course of direction. We really didn't have any certainty that Parker was a sure thing, but we knew God wanted us to take a step of faith without any safety nets! And that we did.

Uh - Oh. Now what? The Colorado church door closed to us. Obviously, God had a different plan or should I say a different dance? God began cultivating what He wanted us to do but, to be brutally honest, I didn't like it. Neither did my husband. We fought God, telling Him that all we wanted to do was to get out of ministry at this point, and live like other people do. We wanted to go back into the workforce and leave all ministry pain behind. Did God listen to us? Absolutely. Did He give us what we insisted we wanted? No. We were both looking for a fresh start and the Colorado Rockies in the west would have been a wonderful, refreshing change. But . . . it wasn't to be. God had a particular plan He wanted birthed.

Gary was serving his last month at the church and during this time God began a full-fledged tugging at his heart to start a new church – yes - one from scratch. We both *told* God we were not interested. Like Moses, our attitude was, *Lord, please get someone else to do this job.* But the Lord knew what He had made us of, the strength he had implanted in us by His Holy Spirit, and our soft, pliable hearts, so He continued to gently pursue our cooperation. And, in the end, we would always choose to submit to what God wanted for our lives.

Gary was now more open to hearing and accepting what God had to say. During one of Gary's prayer times he asked, "God, if we are to start a church, how would it be funded? Where would it meet? What would it look like?" After receiving unquestionable assurance in his heart that God wanted him to start a church, Gary prayed, "I wouldn't even know what to name it." God caused Gary to recall a tattoo he had seen inscribed on Joel's arm. Joel was instrumental in leading our son, Matthew, in his decision to accept Christ as his Savior. Joel's tattoo read, AGAPE. Agape means *God's unconditional love.* This is the name God impressed Gary to name the church.

Gary had now welcomed and embraced the new journey God had planned. His life verse at that time was, *"He has put a new song in my mouth; Praise to our God; Many will see it and fear, and will trust in the Lord."* (Psalm 40:3)

Agape Fellowship Church, York, Pennsylvania, began August 21, 2005. We held our first service in the family room of our home with 37 people. We stayed in our home for several weeks, moved to an available room in a nursing home, then onto a school and finished up in a tiny red brick historic chapel within 12 years.

God enlarged my own ministry several years ago after Agape Fellowship was established. I started a ministry to pastor's wives called 'Safe Haven,' realizing from first-hand experience that due to the unique needs of a life in the ministry, we need each other - colleagues in the same vocation - to share the joys, what we are going through and to lift each other up during the weighty, tearful times.

Safe Haven is a *"green pastures and still waters"* refuge with four to six original and new ladies attending. We meet throughout the year to stay in touch. These ladies are lifesavers for me. I know I can phone, text, email or scream and they will be there for me; and me for them! One friend, Pearl, had been dealing with the difficulty of losing her husband. She was the first in our group to walk this journey of grief. Supporting her however she needed us during this part of her dance is what we do. We have each other's back! That's why we call it *SAFE HAVEN*.

Safe - dwelling without fear or harm
Haven - a sheltered area

"Then they are glad because they are quiet; so, He guides them to their desired haven." (Psalm 107:30)

9

Dance

- Like Riding a Bike -

You Never Forget!

———————————•◆◇—————◈◆•———————————

Backtracking a bit. Shortly after we moved to York, I joined the York Homeschool Network while homeschooling Matt and Josh. This was a real learning chapter in my life, a dance with which I fought God almost daily. During this dance of life, God was teaching me that my children had to come first before anything I wanted to do, even if it was just dishes, laundry and dinner. God had me rearrange my schedule daily, which was not any easy adjustment for me -- at all. I had to die to self every day, which was so painful.

It was at this time, I met a mom, Deb, who told me about her daughter, Alex. Alex was such an exceptional dancer she could have gone to New York City to dance professionally, but rather decided to open a Christian Dance Studio, "Light of Life Performing Arts" in Seven Valleys, Pennsylvania. Deb had mentioned to her daughter that if she was ever in need of a tap teacher one day, that she knew a pastor's wife who used to teach tap. But, when the time came, Alex didn't know how to contact me.

Alex was going to church one Sunday and, as she drove by Twin Lakes Chapel, God impressed on her to attend that church the next Sunday. She had no idea that my husband was the pastor there at the time. After the service, I approached Alex because I had seen her dance in her recital and told her I knew her mom. After talking to her for a couple minutes, she looked at me and said, "You are the pastor's wife who used to teach tap?!!!" I cautiously replied, "Yes,... I did." She proceeded to tell me that she had been trying to find me. I asked, "Why were you trying to find me?" She replied, "Because I need a tap teacher for my studio." I started to laugh, kind of like Sarah in the Bible when she was told she would have a baby in her old age. That is exactly how I felt. Seventeen years had passed since I last taught dance. *Seventeen years!* Well, I told her I would think about it and she invited me to come to the studio and check out a class. I did just that and as I sat watching the class, God began to flood my mind with all kinds of steps and ideas that I could undertake. I jumped up and began to dance again. It was like riding a bike! It was as if I had never stopped. Oh, the bliss!

Now mind you, at this time in my life, I had extreme pain in my lower back, so painful that I couldn't walk without stabbing pains shooting down my legs. I never thought I would dance again! Someone recommended seeing a Chiropractor. I did, and Doctors Kevin and Selina Jackson have been lifesavers in restoring my ability to move. Thankfully, regular chiropractic maintenance has kept me going. So, I can happily report that I have been teaching at LOLPA (Light of Life Performing Arts) since 2003.

I love teaching at this age and enjoy making spiritual deposits into lives through the relationships made by teaching my art.

I remember a conversation I had with my daughter-in-law, Skye, about a show she had just attended at the studio where I teach tap. Skye commented, "I wish I would have taken dance when I was young. It looks like so much fun! I think I am too old to start now." As her words filtered through my mind at lightning speed, I blurted out, "It is NEVER too late to learn to dance!" Some people want to dance but think they can't because they either didn't start when they were young or because they feel it is too late. Not true! Anyone can learn to dance at any age. Always!

Twenty-five years after I *gave it all up*, God returned to me the joy of dancing onstage with the "Mom's Tap Class" at LOLPA. I never thought I would ever be dancing on a stage again. Oh! The familiar thrill of getting ready in costume, makeup and hair! I admit being terribly nervous! It took me back to when I was younger and the tummy butterflies I had every time I danced in a show. I love that my LOLPA students and I dance together in the "Shim Sham Shimmy Tap Finale." I still get excited and thrilled to perform.

Recently, I had the honor of a ZOOM session with Rusty Frank, a legend in tap! She watched my tap dancers perform the National Anthem of Tap, "Shim Sham Shimmy" from the comfort of her home in LA. During our time together, Rusty shared how she has performed in 23 countries around the World teaching tap. We were in awe. She passionately shared, "You never know where your dancing shoes will take you!" I had to pen that in this book. So true! I never thought my tap shoes would end up at the nursing home where my mom resided to dance for the residents to bring smiles to their faces. Maybe I've slowed down a lot and can't kick quite as high as I once could, but I have fun and we all get a good laugh!

I am forever amazed that while teaching the students new steps or when they are learning tap, they tend to look down at their feet thinking this will help them learn the steps faster. I have to remind them to look up and keep their eyes straight ahead. Wow! What a lesson for us! Don't look down, but up! Keep your head lifted high and keep your focus on Christ. I'm reminded of Peter in the Bible who asked Jesus to call him out of the boat to walk to Him. Walk on water? When Jesus granted him to come, Peter never thought twice about it. He stepped out of the boat and looked straight into Jesus' eyes and began to walk on water. The very moment He took his eyes off of Christ was when the sinking began! The same is true in our lives. When we keep our focus on Christ, we can more easily comply with all He asks. But, when we begin to look down and try to weigh the options and rationalize what He is asking, that is when we begin to sink. You may know the hymn "Turn Your Eyes Upon Jesus." The words speak truth to this principle.

"TURN YOUR EYES UPON JESUS"
Helen H. Lemmel

O soul, are you weary and troubled? No light in the darkness you see?
There's light for a look at the Savior, and life more abundant and free!

Turn your eyes upon Jesus, look full in His wonderful face,
And the things of earth will grow strangely dim, In the light of His glory and grace.

Through death into life everlasting, He passed, and we follow Him there;
O'er us sin no more hath dominion—for more than conqu'rors we are!

His Word shall not fail you—He promised; believe Him, and all will be well:
Then go to a world that is dying, His perfect salvation to tell!

Turning our eyes upon Jesus will not only help our spiritual balance it will also help our heart balance. When looking up, this will provide better balance for our dance. Do not look down, but look up! Don't watch your feet.

Ken Gire, in his book The Divine Embrace, states:

"From the missteps in my spiritual life, I have learned a few things about dancing with Jesus. The most important is this: If we fall in love, our feet will follow. If we draw close to Him and stay close, we won't have to worry about our feet or where He may be leading them. That doesn't mean we won't step on His toes. It doesn't mean we won't trip over our own feet. It doesn't mean we won't bump into other people. What it does mean is that Jesus will be with us through all the complicated steps and sudden turns, steadying us if we stumble, picking us up if we fall, and doing whatever it takes to keep us dancing."

You see, there are many dance partners in our journey of life, some for a day, some for a season and some for a lifetime! But each one makes a difference in our dance. The girls I have taken and performed dance with from Jean Kettell Studio of Dance over the years have stayed in touch and we often have a reunion. Sue, Tosha, who choreographs this dance party, Stephanie, Yvonne, Melinda and Sharon, all embrace catching up on life and reminiscing. I have known some for over 60 years! How fun it is to catch up on what is happening in all of our lives! It is always a great time looking back at our albums of pictures and taking a trip down memory lane showcasing our dances, costumes, shows, friend updates and experiences.

Gary had dreams, too! As you know from Chapter 5, Gary's dream of meeting Phil Keaggy came true! But he had another big dream. Gary has always loved turkey hunting more than any other type of hunting. Sometimes I joke, "It is God... turkeys... then me." God used turkey hunting to spare this steelworker, body builder and night-club bouncer - bringing him to salvation in Christ and to become a pastor.

At a point earlier in Gary's life, he developed a friendship with 5X World Champion Turkey Caller, Preston Pittman, from Mississippi. They cultivated a relationship over the phone for 10 years, yet never meeting in person. We had hoped there would come a day when it would be possible for the two to get together. That likelihood would not be easy. BUT GOD!

In March 2023, Gary and Preston met face to face after all those years. Preston was invited to the Genesis Church in York, Pennsylvania, where he was to be their First Outdoor Show main speaker. Gary had a part in orchestrating this Divine opportunity and we hosted Preston at our home for a few days. What a DREAM come true for

*Ken Gire, The Divine Embrace, (Wheaton, IL: Tyndale House Publishers, Inc.), pp. 124-125

Gary! We relished in loud turkey calls, getting to know each other and wild-game meals.

Sometimes we are found lacking, thinking God is not interested in our desires. But... HE IS! So never stop short of dreaming big for God! And if it is in His choreography for you... it will happen!

God loves for us to Ask, Seek and Knock. (Matthew 7:7-12) "Keep on asking and you will receive what you ask for. Keep on seeking and you will find what you're looking for. Keep on knocking, and the door will be opened to you. But even more so, God loves for us to DREAM BIG! Ephesians 3:20 says, *"Now to Him who is able to do exceedingly abundantly above all that we ask or think, according to the power that works in us."*

So, stay focused. Keep your eyes upward and you will find that God will lead you to people and places you would never think of, dream of or ever imagine... in your *sacred dance!*

10
Dance Seasons

"There is a time for everything,
and a season for every activity under the heavens;
a time to be born and a time to die, a time to plant and a time to uproot,
a time to kill and a time to heal, a time to tear down and a time to build,
a time to weep and a time to laugh, a time to mourn and A TIME TO DANCE,
a time to scatter stones and a time to gather them,
a time to embrace and a time to refrain from embracing,
a time to search and a time to give up, a time to keep and a time to throw away,
a time to tear and a time to mend, a time to be silent and a time to speak,
a time to love and a time to hate, a time for war and a time for peace."
(Ecclesiastes 3:1-8)

What do we do when God doesn't look like what we expected? He doesn't do what we thought He should do or how we thought He should do it. Are we able to pray, worship and sing during the tough seasons of the dance? The "Desert Song" is a reminder to me that in all of my life and in every season, God is still God so, I should be able to sing and worship Him through it all – even when a child becomes a prodigal, even when there is an unexpected death in the family, even when there is no end in sight of trials in a marriage and the list goes on. God is there in every season of our lives.

In Romans 8:28, the Bible tells us, *"And we know that all things work together for good to those who love God, to those who are the called according to His purpose."* All things! All things!

When I was a young Christian, I began praying for God to bring "Puzzle Piece" Christians into our family when our children would marry. A puzzle usually takes shape as you begin to place the correct pieces together. My family puzzle wasn't looking like what I thought it would look like; the one in my mind (not the one on the puzzle box). Let me explain.

My prayer for our children was for them to experience all that God had for them in marriage. Because I did not know God in my teen years, nor in the first six years of my marriage, I had a lot of regrets and did not want my children to experience them as well. It was so exciting to pray for my children and wonder who may one day be grafted in to be a part of our family when they would marry.

When my children were younger, I shared with them my experiences and regrets. I did this because I believed God prompted me. Not all parents need to share their past with their children, but because I was speaking in churches, youth groups and at Nicole's college (Lancaster Bible College) I needed to be open with them first.

As Nicole was fast approaching her 26th birthday, she would often ask me, "Mom, do you think God has forgotten me? When will I meet the one God has for me?" I would encourage her and tell her, "God has it all under control." But, after so many of her friends were getting married, Gary and I began to wonder why our wonderful daughter had not yet found someone for herself.

Well, one particular puzzle piece (our daughter's mate) came to us in an unexpected way. While Nicole was working at LBC, she met a student named, Mike. Nicole and Mike began to hang out a lot and really enjoyed their time together. Nicole invited Gary and me to the college for a chapel where Mike would be playing the drums. We met Mike, but to our great surprise, Nicole revealed she was very interested in him as a possible boyfriend/husband. Nicole was 26 and Mike -- a shocking 18 -- an entire 8 years younger than Nicole! My response was, "No Way. This is not what I have been praying for or looking for in a mate for you. He is younger than your youngest brother, Josh."

Well, to say the least, things did not start off with a positive beginning. Nicole and Mike were convinced they should be together but it took a lot of prayer and seeking God for me to be open to this possibility. I wrestled intensely with the thoughts of all I wanted for Nicole: a husband who had a home, made good money and had a great job and bright future so she could quit work, stay at home and have children. *But... God!*

In time, Mike won over our hearts and they have been married many years at this writing. They have a wonderful relationship and marriage. They are best friends! I am thrilled for them and would want no one else for her. I joke about the reason why Nicole had to wait so long to marry – she had to wait for Mike to grow up.

My plans are not always a part of God's dance for my family or me. Sometimes His people and plans enter our lives in covert or unexpected ways! My own expectations have been a real hindrance to my walk with Christ. If I do this, I expect God to do that! Whatever made me think I could bargain with God, or argue with God, or wrestle with God? I have never won a match yet. What makes me think I ever will? The most disappointing times in the seasons of my dance have been when God did not do what I thought He should do. That included in my marriage, our family, our finances, and in our church. How would you define disappointment? Wikipedia defines it as: "feeling of dissatisfaction that follows the failure of expectations or hopes to manifest." Dr. Bill Thrasher defines it this way: "Disappointment is God's way of dimming the glamour of the world and deepening our ability to enjoy Him."

Going DEEP is not always what we want - sometimes we coddle the road of comfort and ease. I have had to make adjustments in my walk with Christ because things have not always turned out the way I thought they would or how I wanted. I had to go back on my knees and seek the Lord. This is how I thought - since Math has proven equations like $1 + 1 = 2$, there must be a formula to the Christian faith as well. If I did what I thought God wanted me to do then He would do what I wanted. Where did I ever get that? It is funny how we perceive God in our thoughts like He is a genie in a bottle at our disposal to do what we want. I thought God owed me special favors because I served Him. I needed to learn God was and *is* in control of the *dance seasons* in our lives – not me.

At one point, I was angry at what God was or was not doing. I did not want to write this book because I did not know what to say. I was so disillusioned with my life, family and church and what was and wasn't happening that I thought, there, God, I am not going to write this book. I was pouting about things not turning out the way I had hoped. There were painful situations in our family as well as in the church my husband was pastoring that made me feel like I just wanted to die! The battle in my mind reverberated with - *God, You say You work **all** things out for our good? What kind of good is this? I don't like this, nor do I want to live like this.*

Attending a conference at the beautiful Sandy Cove Conference Center in Northeast, Maryland, I met Kay Arthur, speaker and Bible teacher of "Precept Ministries." I had the golden opportunity to talk with her one-on-one in the ladies' room.

I need to let you in on something, here, especially due to the fact that my pastor's-wives' friends would be shaking their heads about right now. They know that whenever we go to a seminar or event, *I stalk the speakers.* Yes, I admit it! I have stalked Jill Briscoe, Lois Evans, Rhea Briscoe, Tony Evans and, yes, Kay Arthur. I walked into the ladies' room waiting to get her alone after observing that she was not surrounded by people. I timed my bladder break perfectly to wash hands next to her. Ouch! There it is. It is out! My dear friend, Pearl, a pastor's wife at the time, had a t-shirt specially made for me. It read: *I am a Stalker!* and I was to wear it to events to help the speakers watch out for me. Ha-ha.

Recently my friends Tami and Robin stalked out Danny Gokey at an event with me. Because we wanted to get a groupie shot before he walked on stage, his goliath security man told us we could not at that time. Danny came from behind the curtain and told the man in charge to allow the photo before he leaped on stage for his performance. We were thrilled! All humility and no pride.

Well, back to the story.

By invitation from Kay, I had the privilege to attend a "Youniquely You Conference" in Chattanooga, Tennessee, in October 2006. While at the conference, I purchased the book authored by Kay, "AS SILVER REFINED – Learning to Embrace Life's Disappointments." I picked it up because of the timely impact of its title. Kay hand-signed the book for me, but I didn't read it right away. Trusting in God's Sovereignty is the theme throughout the book. I thought I understood this principle until life began to challenge my thinking in how much I believed about God and His goodness during the more difficult seasons of life.

In 2010, I was ready to pick up Kay's book, which I had purchased years before while attending the "Youniquely You Conference." After reading and praying through the study book that partners with the original book, I began to see God's workings in a whole new way. I was no longer mad at God and began taking my circumstances *as they are*, not what I wish they were. I had a whole new attitude adjustment. I had to take every thought captive to achieve victory over the flood of disappointments and disillusionment. My life has changed immensely. I believe I was stuck in a trap by Satan that kept me from trusting God with my husband, family and church. My life's dance included entertaining and dancing through self-pity, the things I felt I should have by now, what I thought God owed me and being overly self-focused. I also dove into the book of Job to get God's perspective on suffering through a righteous man's life.

Reading through the daily devotional, "Discovering God's Daily Agenda," by Henry and Richard Blackaby was timely. The devotion for the 5th of March, "Lessons from the Book of Job," became God's providential timing as both my Bible reading and devotion collided with the same message to me.

"Lessons from the Book of Job"

"But when I looked for good, evil came upon me; And when I waited for light, then came darkness. (Job 30:26)
Job was bewildered. He lived righteously and lived with compassion, but he received God's apparent punishment rather than His blessing. Why do the wicked prosper and good suffer? Few questions vex the thoughtful soul more than this one.
Consider the truths: God is infinitely more righteous than we are. He is not obligated to justify His actions to us. His ways are perfect; ours are not. (Job 4:17)
God targets the pride in our lives because pride convinces us that we don't need Him. Such thinking is not only false, it's dangerous, so God vigorously opposes it. (Job 10:16)
Some wicked men live long; seemingly contented lives while some good men suffer misery and die young. (Job 21:25)
There is clearly no set formula for the way God deals with people. God challenges Job's credentials for judging the way He is ruling the universe. (Job 40:4)

We are no more qualified than Job to question God's ways. The book of Job reveals that God will allow the righteous to endure affliction, but He will never forsake us. (Job 8:20; Job 19:25) God's redemptive purposes far exceed our desire for comfort."

Well said! What makes me think God owes me anything? Honestly, Heaven should be enough! I have an American mindset that makes me feel I deserve or am entitled! It is all around me. Do what you want when you want and you do not need to answer to anyone! God, please forgive me. May God be praised through each season of my life, my family and my church.

"DESERT SONG"
Hillsong UNITED

Bridge
All of my life in every season
You are still God
I have a reason to sing
I have a reason to worship

"People are about as happy as they make up their minds to be." (Abraham Lincoln)

11
Dance Routine of Life

Circumstances in our lives are the dance lessons; the mundane and routine of daily life are where we live. The great evangelist, Billy Graham, observed, *"Mountaintops are for the view and inspiration, but fruit is grown in the valleys."* We do not live on the mountaintop as much as we would like to, but exist in the daily grind of health issues, bills, children, family crisis, shopping, laundry, meals, etc. When out of our control (by the way, most of life is) we need to choose to *rely on God* to order our steps for the *dance routine of life*. My husband, Gary, coined the phrase, "You'll never enjoy the dance while always watching your feet!" So true.

Sometimes I hear God in a gentle small voice and other times He needs to yell loud and clear: *Trust Me; trust Me! – Lean not; lean not to your own understanding. Let Me lead! Stop trying to be the Holy Spirit to your husband, children and church. Um . . . you're leading again!*

Recently, I was attending a wedding in our church over which Gary was officiating. During the reception swing dance lessons were offered. The newlyweds had met at a swing-dance club. This is very popular in the York, and Lancaster, Pennsylvania, areas. It was tons of fun watching couples enter the dance floor dressed in 1940's attire with bow ties, suits, halter-styled dresses and spiked heels. They were as smooth as any dancers I had ever seen. It was clean fun!

Well, I had never attempted swing dancing before, so I joined the dance floor for the lesson. They had all the men line up as the lead dancers on the right and the girls as followers to the left. Since my partner was the groom's mother, I took the lead. I was the only woman on the men's side. Surprising, huh? I had tried earlier to follow a young man's lead in dancing and struggled to even get started and gracefully bowed off the dance floor. I just had to lead! So, with the instruction, we were off and running and having a grand old time! I learned once again; I have trouble following. I want to lead. This is my personal struggle with God. I need to back off and let Him have His rightful place and believe He is able to do far more than I could think, dream or imagine! Emma, a former tap student of mine said, "Sometimes I think: why did I choose dance? Then I realize I didn't choose dance at all. Dance chose me." I can identify with this quote from Emma. Dance was implanted into my own heart from my earliest memory!

What freedom comes when you know the steps of a dance and can perform it without thinking about it! You are free to relax and comfortably do what you have trained for. You are like a well-oiled machine! It is so much fun! *Let's have fun!* We only get one life, here.

How are you doing in your *dance routine of life?* Are you trying to lead? Do you need to step back and trust God to choreograph your dance? Have you made a mess of your dance? God is perfectly able, and more than able, to design your dance. Get out of

God's way! Stop trying to lead the dance!

> *"You have turned my mourning into dancing; You have put off my sackcloth and clothed me with gladness, to the end that my glory may sing praise to You and not be silent. O, LORD my God, I will give thanks to You forever."*
> *(Psalm 30:11-12)*

Cathy, a dear friend, sent me an article via email from Crosswalk.com; "Girlfriends in God" devotion, Wednesday, September 17, 2008; Mrs. Jayne's: "You're Leading Again." (Condensed)

> *"After ten years of marriage, I convinced my very masculine husband to take ballroom dance classes with me. The first order of business at our initial ballroom dance class was to learn the Fox Trot. "Okay, Dr. and Mrs. Jaynes," the instructor began, "today, we will learn a dance called the Fox Trot. Dr. Jaynes, you place your right hand on your wife's left shoulder blade. Cup it firmly in your hand." Then she turned to me. "Now, Mrs. Jaynes, you gently rest your left hand on your husband's right shoulder." So far so good, we all agreed. "Dr. Jaynes, you have the hardest part because the man has to learn how to lead. All the woman has to do is follow." More than once she tapped me on the shoulder and said, "Mrs. Jaynes, you're leading again." I had wanted to feel like Ginger Rogers, gliding in graceful movements across the dance floor but, instead, I felt like a shopping buggy being pushed through the supermarket, and Steve looked more like Fred Rogers instead of Fred Astaire. All the while, I was being reprimanded, "Mrs. Jaynes, you're leading again." Another thing we learned; we had to learn to not look down at our feet, but at each other. "Concentrate on looking at each other's face," the instructor said. "Looking at your feet will not make them do the right steps. You need to listen to the music and let your feet move around the room." Yeah, right, I thought. I felt better looking down, as if my eyes could will my feet into the correct steps. Eventually, however, I did learn to keep my eyes off my feet and on my handsome leader's face."*

The application of this lesson shows the beauty of giving control over to God, but it is also a picture of the beauty of a marriage when the husband is the spiritual leader.

Life is a Dance and God is *the* Choreographer and since I am a Christian, I realize that this life is His dance, not mine, to write. He will choreograph it as I let go. I am to just follow His lead and dance. Why do I think God needs my advice or help in His Choreography? Who am I? But I still try to tell God what to do or what I think is best from time to time.

"LIFE'S A DANCE"
John Michael Montgomery

When I was fourteen, I was fallin' fast
For a blue-eyed girl in my homeroom class.
Tryin' to find the courage to ask her out
Was like tryin' to get oil from a water spout.
What she would've said, I can't say.
I never did ask then she moved away.

I learned something from my blue-eyed girl:
sink or swim, you gotta give it a whirl.

Life's a dance, you learn as you go.
Sometimes you lead, sometimes you follow.
Don't worry 'bout what you don't know,
life's a dance, you learn as you go.

The longer I live the more I believe
You do have to give if you wanna receive.
There's a time to listen, a time to talk.
And you might have to crawl even after you walk.
Had sure things blow up in my face,
Seen the longshot win the race.
Been knocked down by the slammin' door.
Picked myself up and came back for more.

Life's a dance - Life's a dance - Life's a dance
Take a chance on love
Life's a dance - you learn as you go

We need to remember that we do learn as we go. We are not responsible for anyone's dance but our own. Go with God through life and let Him lead the Daily Dance Routine!

12
The Dance Performance

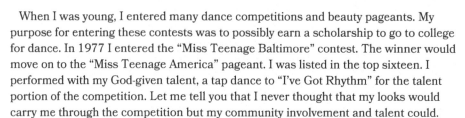

When I was young, I entered many dance competitions and beauty pageants. My purpose for entering these contests was to possibly earn a scholarship to go to college for dance. In 1977 I entered the "Miss Teenage Baltimore" contest. The winner would move on to the "Miss Teenage America" pageant. I was listed in the top sixteen. I performed with my God-given talent, a tap dance to "I've Got Rhythm" for the talent portion of the competition. Let me tell you that I never thought that my looks would carry me through the competition but my community involvement and talent could.

At the end of the pageant before they announce the winner, they bring all the girls on stage to hand out two awards: the "Miss Congeniality Award" and the "Miss Leadership Award." Well, I didn't think that I would qualify for either of those, so I pretty much checked-out while they were going through the process. Mind you that this contest was not a little to-do. We had young girls represented from each county accompanied by their families. The event was being video-taped. Wow! This was a big deal in 1977! As they announced the name for the "Miss Congeniality Award," I was in a fog. Did I just hear my name? Oh, my! It couldn't be. All the girls looked at me and – me at them. Why? Well, because I was the last person that would have qualified for the kindest, nicest person award. You see, I was there to win and in the beauty contest world it can be dog-eat-dog.

I took my step down off the riser and proceeded in shock to the emcee to collect my trophy. In a daze during that foggy walk, I was saying to myself... *I didn't vote for me, why would anyone else?* I put one foot in front of the other to complete the longest walk of my life – my victory lap on the runway -- then turned around and walked back to my spot on the riser. I just know as I walked to the presenters that the girls were pondering in their puzzled minds, *you've got to be kidding!* Well, they proceeded to read the name for the "Miss Leadership Award." "OOPS! We have made a mistake!" Oh, my, gosh; what now? "The 'Miss Leadership Award' goes to Cheryl Kyte [nee]." Okay! I can handle that. That made more sense because of my community involvement and leadership skills. So, I had to take a second lap around the runway!

Sometimes in life we compete against each other, even in the church world. I wish I had the gift of singing, preaching, serving the homeless, giving, but God decides and disperses spiritual gifts to us; we do not choose them. On Earth, we are not in a competition to perform for God or for an earthly prize. My precious prize provided for me is my personal relationship with Jesus Christ and the gifts He has entrusted to me. But of highest value - my salvation and eternity in Heaven!

Don't try to perform another's dance; embrace your own. This is not always easy – when you yearn for a life partner and it seems like God has you on delay; or you have lost a spouse and you don't know where to turn next; or perhaps you have been trying to conceive and everyone else around you is getting pregnant and you aren't. Life has its share of twists and turns and the dance is more than just steps. Remember, God doesn't ask us to choreograph the steps to the dance or to understand them right now. He asks us to take His hands and follow Him! He sees the bigger picture and knows what is ahead. Ken Gire says in his book Divine Embrace:

". . . the Christian life is more about intimacy, not technique. The Lord of the dance doesn't want us to worry about our feet. He doesn't want us wondering about the steps ahead. He merely wants us to feel the music, fall into His arms and follow His Lead."

How are you doing in your dance of life? Are you trying to lead? Do you need to step back and trust God to choreograph your dance? He is perfectly able to lead your dance and do a much better job than you can do.

Maybe you would say, "I don't know how to dance. I have two left feet. I am not coordinated at all." You don't have to know how to dance to participate in your God-directed dance. It is God's responsibility to teach you to dance. God is asking us to take His hand and follow His lead. He is calling to us in His quiet, small, gentle voice, *Shall We Dance?*

Since I was age three, my life consisted of performing for people from the safe, microscopic living room to immense arena-size stages. I loved being in the spotlight! It was where I could escape any earthly problems. Shining like a star with the sparkles, sequins and fringes was my bright spot in life. After I became a Christian, I took the performance trap into what I did for God.

God is not a formula, a plan or a method. He is a Person! Guess how long it took me to realize this? I admit – almost twenty-eight years of being a Christian. Some of us cannot seem to grasp this when we first become a believer. For years I wanted to *dance for* God for the purpose of finding fulfillment by trying to please Him. I was bound by chains of duty and performance under the deception that I needed to do something for God in order to repay Him for what He did for me. If there was no act or deed I could perform to earn a place in Heaven *before* I accepted the Lord, then why would I think I needed to perform for God *after* I knew Him? I think most Christians struggle with the misconception that they need to continue to *do things* in their Christian walk in order to maintain God's approval. Evangelist, Rev. Billy Graham, taught the Biblical foundation that, "Your salvation depends on what Christ has done for you, not on what you can do for Him," whether it is when you first received your salvation or thinking you have to work to keep it. What a shock when we finally grasp that God does not want us to *do anything!*

This may not sit well with some because of varying spiritual upbringings. I completely understand! I still meditate on and am working to fully embrace this wonderfully liberating aspect of God. God loves me, accepts me and assures me my place in Heaven by one fact alone: I have received His Son. I cannot *do* one thing to make Him love me more, nor can I lessen His love or cause Him to think less of me whenever I do, say or think something wrong.

This is the *dance of grace*. It is like no other! Oh, the freedom we experience in our Christian walk when true grace is embraced! My days of performing to stay approved are over! Hallelujah! My dance performance for acceptance is complete! It was finished through Christ's death on the cross on the day I confessed Jesus as my Lord and Savior in April 1985. God loves me just the way I am. I just never comprehended that! I no longer want to dance to the same old tune!

After reading Bill Gillham's "Lifetime Guarantee - Making Your Christian Life Work and What To Do When It Doesn't," my thinking was challenged and changed from the law that I placed myself under to understanding my identity in Christ, who I really am, and embracing it!

The good news! – Check out these reassuring Scriptures.

- *I am fully pleasing to my Father. (Colossians 2:13), (Romans 3:27), (Romans 4:2)*
- *I already have a place reserved for me in Heaven. (Ephesians 2:6)*
- *I am already accepted by Jesus. (Romans 15:7)*
- *Because of Jesus, God counts me as perfect (complete) in relationship with Him. (Colossians 2:10).*
- *I am no longer burdened by the laborious, impossible rules of religious law! If we could grasp this, the true understanding of grace, we could experience the abundant life God designed for each of us in this dance of life!*
- *Is the law then against the promises of God? Certainly not! For if there had been a law given which could have given life, truly righteousness would have been by the law. But the Scripture has confined all under sin, that the promise by faith in Jesus Christ might be given to those who believe. (Galatians 3:21-22)*

The burden of the law strips away life and is death. But grace (through Jesus Christ) is life and living. Christian author, Steve McVey, addresses the *law* and *performance* this way.

"It is important to remember that living by the law doesn't necessarily mean that you focus on the law found in Scripture. Like the Pharisees, many people have gone beyond the Bible and created their own laws. A lifestyle ruled by law is one where the focus is on performance. It is a lifestyle which is obsessed with doing the right thing instead of being obsessed with Jesus."

**"When the law rules a Christian, his focus is on improving his behavior. Yet even if he does manage to improve his behavior, what has he accomplished spiritually? Even an unsaved person can often improve his performance. Jesus didn't give the gift of salvation merely to help us perform better. He came to earth so that we might have an abundant life! (John 10:10). There are many miserable Christians who have exemplary behavior, but joy doesn't come by doing the right thing. In a lifestyle where the grace rules, Jesus is the source of joy."*

This describes my life and dance performance for most of my Christian life. I wasn't aware I was thinking this way. I was convinced I was doing all the right things! So, what fruit did this produce in my life? Major negative responses. I was the judge of my life and - of others. So ugly! So deceptive! I didn't consciously realize I was doing this.

*Steve McVey, Grace Rules, (Eugene, Oregon: Harvest House Publishers), p. 70
**Steve McVey, Grace Rules, (Eugene, Oregon: Harvest House Publishers), p. 73

I was so focused on the law of right and wrong and my own behavior that I thought I not only needed to, but I could improve me more and more. And then – why couldn't others do the same? If I allot more time with Jesus: pray, read, church attendance, get involved in Christian things, I would attain! That is why I say God is not a formula, plan or method. He is a Person to have a relationship with... through Jesus Christ.

As I have previously revealed, I was a person who robbed the sacred gift of the life of my child and obliterated it from existence. But God, in His unfailing love, rescued me from my sin and guilt. I tried to perform for God for a long time, since I felt He had rescued me from such a heinous crime. I danced for years to repay God. Then, one freeing day, when I truly understood God's unconditional grace and forgiveness given to me – out of the bondage of my own chains and those the enemy had used to knot me up, I was set free to live an unabashed, shameless dance! I danced, now, because I realized I already had His approval all along!

The word "*tetelestai*" means "it is finished" in the Greek language. These are the words Jesus cried out on the cross! No more doing, no more trying, no more performance to win His acceptance! Who could top His performance anyway? Living in God's true grace -- what a way to love and live in Christ!

To read more about God's grace, I recommend these four books:

Steve McVey (Harvest House)
Grace Walk
Grace Rules
Amazing Grace
Bill Gillham (Harvest House)
Lifetime Guarantee

When you experience the freedom to dance for God because you want to minister to Him (Ezekiel 44:9-26, 28, 31; Luke 17:7-10), it can feel as if the only people in existence are you and Him! After 24 years of knowing Christ, I performed an interpretive dance; an act of worship and abandonment. It was unparalleled exhilaration!

"Your feet can learn the steps, but only your spirit can do the dance."
(Author unknown)

God longs for us to be free in our dance. As we turn control over to God there is joy and freedom in the dance. The freedom of the dance is in following Christ's lead. He dances so naturally and moves so fluidly that sometimes we don't even have time to think about where He is taking us. Wherever He is taking us, though, there are things He wants to show us along the way, experiences He wants to share with us, words He wants to speak to us. At various turns on the dance floor, there is grace He wants to extend to others through us.

Our assurance for the guidance we need is not on our education, however excellent it may be. It is not in our experience, however extensive. It is not even in our gifting, however extraordinary. Our assurance is in the arm he has around us. He wants us to feel the firmness of that arm, to trust in its sureness, and to have the music of His voice become such a part of us . . . that we can almost forget about our feet."

Wow, what freedom comes when you know the steps of the dance and perform without even thinking? Shear abandonment! We only get one life; let's forget about our feet. Let's dance like no one is watching!

CHURCH MUSIC – "Dance"
David Crowder Band

Dance if you're wounded, Dance if you're torn in two
Dance broken open, Dance with nothing to lose

(Oh!) Perfectly free
(Oh!) Dance if you wanna be
(Oh!) Perfectly free
(Oh!) Dance if you wanna be

Change the world - Change your soul
Fill it up - Here we go - Here we go

Oh, His is a story that saves, Majestic feel
Feel it at a steady pace

Divine Embrace; Ken Gire; p 99

13
Don't Give Up -
God is Working Behind
the Curtain

When you feel ready to give up the dance -- *Don't be so quick!* I was so dreadfully tired of thinking about the book and trying to get someone to tell me if they thought anyone would even be interested in reading it. For years I spent endless days gathering myriads of post-it notes and scattered scrap pieces of notepaper to draft a chapter here and there. I asked several people to read what I had written hoping to discover perhaps that one of them might be interested in editing my book. But, to no avail!

Then, one day on an unplanned trip to my favorite store, Bon Ton, I dropped in to see my friend Betsy Beck, who had previously hired me for seasonal work one Christmas. She asked me how my book was going. I was quite surprised that she had remembered I was writing a book. I told her I was ready to give it up; I couldn't find an editor. She said she had a friend who would be perfect for editing the book and said she would contact her for me to see if she might be interested. When I left the office, I didn't expend any energy thinking about it any further, because I had previously had so many people say the same thing but whom never got back to me.

A couple of days later, I was actually introduced to Betsy's friend, Deb Hamilton, who contacted me. Editing began immediately! Since that God-arranged introduction, we have had a relationship through e-mail and Facebook and I didn't know her voice and would not have been able to pick her face out in a mall. Ten months into the editing process, God blessed us with the opportunity to meet face to face and she has been an ongoing inspiration to help me tell "my story!" God knew what I needed, when I needed Deb and how He would use me in her life as well. How did God confirm to me that He wanted my book written? Deb's side of the story lets us in on it.

Deb had been plugging away at the editing process for some time when one day she sent me the following note.

> "Hi, Cheryl. Two days before Betsy introduced us — put us together via Facebook — I had just finished helping to edit my brother-in-law's book, gratis. I immediately prayed that night: "Father, you know I need to bring some income into our home for our bills and I need a job I can do in my home because of where we live now. You know there are no jobs in this area. You also know, Lord, how much I love to edit, but there's no way for anyone to know who I am, what I do, and how to contact me. Only a few people know

what I do. You know I can't afford to advertise. How will anyone ever find me to do editing? Please make a way."

Betsy and I have been very close friends for many years, but due to my husband's job, we were forced to relocate out-of-state. Because of the natural evolution of moving away, it would be months and months between Betsy's and my communication and we hadn't talked in a long time at this point. When Betsy contacted me two days after I had prayed my prayer about God providing me with an editing job, I literally almost buckled to the floor! It shocked me so much that the Lord had heard and answered my prayer so very fast, that I almost had to keep pinching myself to believe it was actually real — I was just so absolutely stunned (we shouldn't be)! It was a real miracle to me.

Even when we were put together, I'm sure you had many other options and didn't have to choose me for the job. I appreciate this opportunity to work with you and to sculpt your book to be as beautiful as possible. God put out his hand to me and led me in this very happy, unexpected dance. Thank you for trusting me with this. Hugs, Deb"

God took two women, who didn't know each other, lived states away from each other, whose needs fit together like a hand in a glove and connected them to bless them both and to accomplish His will — the book. Part of an added blessing to this God-directed collaboration is that Deb has been a pastor's wife for many years, so she understands ministry life as well, which further benefited this book's editing process. We are vocational peers.

Though the wait seemed grueling to find an editor, and I almost gave up what I felt God wanted me to do, God was working undercover on arrangements all along to fuse the right connection — choreographing a new dance for a new performance.

Writing does not come easy to me, but Deb has made this journey delightful as we knit our hearts together over Messenger and Emails. I would prefer to tap dance in front of a million people before penning my memoir, but God would not let me go!

King David encourages us to always *wait* for the Lord. And, he had an abundance of experience in the area of waiting on the Lord.

- *"Wait for the Lord; be strong and take heart and wait for the Lord."* (Psalm 27:14)
- *"Lord, I wait for You; You will answer, Lord my God." (Psalm 38:15)*
- *"I wait for the Lord, my whole being waits, and in His word I put my hope." (Psalm 130:5)*

God sees every detail of your life right now. He is always working behind the scenes on your behalf. Even when it seems like a long delay, don't give up. You're just doing a slow dance right now. Keep holding on. Wait on the Lord.

"And I am certain that God, who began the good work within you, will continue His work until it is finally finished on the day when Christ Jesus returns."
(Philippians 1:6)

14
Who Told Me I Can't Dance

"REMIND ME WHO I AM"
Jason Gray

When I lose my way,
And I forget my name, Remind me who I am.
In the mirror all I see, is who I don't wanna be, remind me who I am.
In the loneliest places, when I can't remember what grace is.

Tell me once again who I am to You.
Who I am to You.
Tell me - must I forget who I am to You.
That I belong to You . . . to You.

When my heart is like a stone,
And I'm running far from home, Remind me who I am.
When I can't receive your love, afraid I'll never be enough, remind me who I am.
If I'm your beloved . . . can you help me believe it.

I had dealt with a serious physical issue as a child. From nine years old until I was a freshman in high school, there was a pitch-black time in my dance. This included doctors, EEG's, medicine, a spinal tap and separation from my parents.

In one day, my dance changed. Playing hide-and-seek at my next-door neighbor's home with Patty and Chris (sisters), I decided the best place to hide was under a table. Upon them spotting me, I sprang up under the hard wooden table and banged my head as I tried to get out of the confined space. As soon as I got to my feet, my words started slurring. The blank look on my face scared my friends, so they ran to get Miss Marianne, their mom. Miss Marianne was a nurse so, right away, she knew after sitting me down on the chair that I was having a seizure. My face was twitching on the left side as drool was coming out of my mouth and my face and speech were uncontrollable. My friends dashed to get my mother. We lived in a neighborhood of brick rowhomes (now called townhomes), so the only thing my friends had to do was jump over the fence. I can only imagine what went through my mother's mind. As she approached me, I tried to talk, but words did not make sense to her or me. This began a rollercoaster of a dance for the next six years.

"Dr. Livingston, I presume." Who would've known I'd have my own encounter with a

Dr. Livingston? It sort of made me chuckle inside. But he was a scary man to look at and his doctor's office in downtown Baltimore was even more frightening. After visiting with the doctor upstairs, they took me downstairs into a dark wire-caged area where they placed me on a bed, gave me medicine to make me sleepy, began placing what I would call goop on my head and then attached special sensors, called electrodes, to my scalp. The electrodes produced a reading to the nurse about my electrical brain activity and generated a paper printout showing wavy lines that would indicate the normal or changing behavior of the brain. EEGs were one of the best procedures used to confirm a diagnosis of seizures. I tried so hard to fall asleep, but think about it - a scary, dark environment, a hard table as a bed, my head hooked up to a machine and noises I've never heard before.

The routine played out by this procedure went this way. After I did fall asleep, they called my name and asked me to open my eyes and to keep them open while they flashed the brightest light in my face – the brightest I have ever seen. My eyes would generate tears from the intense light. Then they began a strobe light effect and kept telling me to keep my eyes open. Sometimes seizures can be triggered by flashing lights and stress. When I was finished, I could not wash my hair, so my mom brought a bandana for me to cover my hair. I think this was more embarrassing than the actual procedure. I guess my vanity started young.

During this dark time in my dance, I went to Johns Hopkins Hospital for a spinal tap and when they didn't insert the needle into the correct location the first time, I cringed in pain. This is the reason I had opted for natural childbirth with my three kiddos; I didn't want another needle piercing my spine. I was also placed on Phenobarbital for the seizure's diagnosis. This drug slows down the activity of your brain and nervous system and is used to treat or prevent seizures. Three times a day I needed to remember to take my medication. Dr. Livingston believed that I had a mild case of epilepsy. He explained that there was a nerve ending in my brain that was not fused where it needed to be and when I hit my head on the table, it discharged a shock to this vulnerable area of my brain.

So, I became marked as a child with epilepsy. Throughout all the years of this diagnosis, I was in and out of the hospital and doctors' offices. After my eighth-grade year in junior high school (that is what it was called back then), upon entering into my high school experience, I was released from the doctors' oversight since I didn't have more than three occurrences and I seemed to be better. This was a tremendous weight off my shoulders going into high school as I am sure it was for my parents also. Praise the Lord! It was a miracle that I could dance as well as I did with the medication. That was God helping me in my dance!

But – what does it look like when we can no longer dance? In 2011 after saying yes to the Haiti missions' trip, I experienced more than my fair share of health issues. After 50-plus years of great health and an occasional ding, it was the most physically challenging year I have ever been through. I think when your health and physical ability to function in your own normal capacity is hindered, it can affect everything. For me, it affected my mind and attitude to the point that everyone around knew that *something was wrong*. I know our physical anatomy was not made to live forever and our bodies are a constant reminder that the *dance* will not last forever, at least here on earth – thank You, God! My prayer: "Let me dance until the day I die!

Jason Gray's song "Remind Me Who I Am" is more than mere words. When we do lose our way – and occasionally we do -- we have to be reminded that God will continue to lead us in the dance. He will be faithful to complete the dance. It may be a dance in a nursing home, or living with your children because you cannot live alone, maybe assisted living, or extreme health challenges, or it could also come in the form of a broken heart from the loss of a loved one. I feel the heartache for so many of those around us, especially those who are dealing with the loss of a loved one.

Loss can impose itself on us in many other forms. My personal challenge and journey of not being able to physically dance and teach was born through the diagnosis of a torn meniscus in my left knee; flat feet that needed inserts, Morton's Neuroma in my left foot, a pedicure that resulted in Cellulitis of the toe resulting in toenail removal, and a skin cancer on my face that needed MOH's surgery. All this took its toll on me within a period of one year.

There were days when I couldn't even get out of bed. And since my usual demeanor in the morning is "So Rise, Shine and Give God the Glory," my husband knew, as did I, something was wrong. This began to weigh my heart and mind down. I was literally in pain just getting out of bed. So, to think I had the rest of the day to walk was overwhelming to me.

I was thankful for my beautiful canine family member, a German Shorthaired female, Bailey. Bailey came to me when I was going through the early stages of menopause. A time of depression descended upon me as the kids were leaving home, getting married and life was changing as I knew it. I had a deep yearning to "nurture." My babies were all grown up and I needed to be needed again as a *mother*. So, we went on a hunt for the perfect dog. My friend, Flo, said, "God sometimes comes in fur," meaning that He uses animals or pets for a need in our lives. Bailey was an addition to my dance that brightened each day*!* She got me up every day to walk her and she had been a motivation to *keep going*! Bailey loved unconditionally and inspired me, comforted me and stayed the course of 13 years with me until the day she passed.

After having the knee surgery, I had inserts placed in my shoes, my toe taped so I did not have to undergo foot surgery, my nail was growing back on the pedicure toe, my face was still healing, and I was getting back to an exercise routine that was helping me shed the weight I gained while dealing with all of the health issues. Health is so important. This was a dance, the magnitude of which I had not been challenged by before. But I know the journey and dance ahead has the potential of becoming more challenging as I get older. My mother-in-law, Dolores (home in Heaven), once said, "Don't grow old; it is not for the faint hearted!" Truth.

Sometimes when I begin to get overwhelmed thinking about the future and the impediment of mobility that I am already experiencing at my age (63 at this time), I begin to get anxious. God has to calm me down and I have to remind myself through God's Word that I will be able to handle what comes my way, because He is my dance partner and will lead me through it all!

One of my heroes is my grandmother, Madeline Carter. She is now *dancing* with the Lord after a lifespan of 97 years. She always had a great outlook, upbeat spirit and kept moving. She not only inspired me, but all of her nine children and spouses, 17 grandchildren, 30 great-grandchildren and great-great grandchildren and one great, great, great grandchild!

I read a very encouraging article in our local newspaper. The article spotlighted a woman who was, at the time of the article, still dancing at 100 years of age. Gladys passed away in 2014.

"Gladys Townsend-Ensor always danced every dance, from the first to the last. When she was younger, people knew where to find her.

Townsend-Ensor turned 100 years old Jan. 14, but her age hasn't stopped her from moving to the music. She and her 78-year-old husband, Phil Ensor, go dancing at clubs all over south-central Pennsylvania two or three times a week. They hit the Valencia Ballroom, the Dillsburg American Legion, the Out Door Country Club and the Gettysburg American Legion whenever there's a big band playing.

Gladys' dad taught her to dance when she was a little girl. She said she always played by herself and that she didn't have shoes or nice clothes. Her dad worked in Pittsburgh and wasn't around much. When he was, he'd take her hand and say, 'Come on, now, Gladys. You're going to dance.'

Her favorite song is "Satin Doll" by Duke Ellington.

She can't walk more than 50 feet. She and Phil Fox Trot to only half of a song before sitting one out. They skip the slow songs, which Gladys doesn't like, anyway.

She married four times. She divorced her first husband, and the following two died - from what, she doesn't quite remember.

When Gladys was in her 80s, she swore off marriage. She said her husbands ignored her. After her third husband died, she spent her evenings reading the Bible.

Then came New Year's Eve 1996, and she needed a date to a dance. She remembered Phil, an acquaintance who was recently widowed. She looked up his number in the phone book and asked him to go. She couldn't get over how handsome Phil looked in his black tux. She said people stared at them on the dance floor, as if they had been together before.

"We danced like we danced our whole lives - like we never missed a step," Gladys said.

They married the following August and spent the next 14 and a half years traveling to Belgium, South America, Florida and Alaska.

They spent their time dancing. "That was the beginning, and this is the end," Gladys said.

She said she didn't find real love until she met Phil and that she thanks him every morning and night for all he does for her. She prays to God for more time. When Gladys' memory gets spotty, Phil pieces together what he can. She said that's the thing about turning 100 - there's so much she can't remember.

Gladys said there's always someone who wants to dance with her, but she only dances with Phil these days. He doesn't want her to fall." (Daily Record; Sunday News; by Leigh Zaleski -- 02/21/2012 09:08:53 AM—EST)

Wow! If that is not inspirational! Just think of her dance and the dances of all her husbands. That's crazy!

Recently, while reading the obituary section of our local newspaper, I was struck by the words written to express the life of Linda M. Oakley from Charleston, SC. The lady said to her husband:

"If it ever hits the fan and I can no longer set you straight about what's amiss in the world, enjoy our evening cocktail hour together, and lovingly kiss you goodnight, call the hospice doc. I'm probably leaving the dance floor."
"Typical Linda Marie Oakley. She danced as long and as fast as she could for the last years of her life while pancreatic cancer did its best to slow her step. It ultimately prevailed but the grace of Linda's step never changed, not even when she tapped her last toe on January 31, 2013 at the Hospice Center of Charleston." (*The York Daily Record; Monday, February 4, 2013)

The funny thing about this is, I never read the obituary section, but the word dance caught my eye. I would love for such words to be said of me until my final breath.

If you think about it, there have got to be health benefits from the activity of dancing. AARP seems to think Dance makes a difference on the longevity of life.

Dancing the Years Away

"Women outnumber men 320 to 150 at Edgewater Pointe, a <u>retirement</u> facility in Boca Raton, Fla. But more ladies are able to cut a rug these days, thanks to paid and volunteer dance partners. Hewitt Bruce, 58, a former cruise ship performer, says the physical benefits outweigh the $20 an hour he gets paid to cha-cha: "The more I <u>dance</u> ... the more I know I am helping preserve the quality of a person's life." <u>AARP BULLETIN</u> | April 1, 2011 (("Dancing preserves quality of life for those at Boca Raton retirement facility." —John W. Adkisson)

I want to dance until the day I die – or should I say pass into the glory of Heaven! I want to dance like there is no tomorrow no matter what age God graces me with on this side of Heaven. Who told me I can't dance?

"KEEP ON DANCING"
(Theme song for "Barbie in the Pink Shoes")
Jim Dooley, Gabriel Mann and Rob Hudnut

I follow my heart, somehow it always seems to know
And when I dance, my feet are dreaming
I close my eyes and let it go, the music flows through me
And then I know I'll be fine

I stretch for the sky, that's where I wanna go
I close my eyes, to see more clearly
The less I think, the more I know
The music flows through me, and then I know I'll be fine

I color outside the lines; I'm changing up all the rhymes
I trip and stumble again, again (again and again)
But at least these steps are mine; even when I fall I shine
I know this feeling will lead me to a bright tomorrow

Listen to the beat of your heart
Keep on dancing - Keep on dancing
Shining just as bright as a star (You're as bright as a star)
Keep on dancing - Keep on dancing
'Cause dance is who I am; dance is who I am

15
The Dance with the Devil

———— •◦◊ — ◊◦• ————

This song and a video of the people in Haiti led me to experience this chapter.

"FOLLOW ME"
Leeland

You lived among the least of these
The weary and the weak
And it would be a tragedy for me to turn away.

All my needs You have supplied.
When I was dead You gave me life.
How could I not give it away so freely?

And I'll follow You into the homes that are broken.
Follow You into the world.
Meet the needs for the poor and the needy, God.
Follow You into the World.

Use my hands, use my feet
To make Your kingdom come
Through the corners of the earth until Your work is done

'Cause Faith without works is dead
And on the cross Your blood was shed
So how can I not give it away so freely?

I give all myself - I give all myself
I give all myself... to You.

This chapter has been the most difficult one for me to write. It may be the most misunderstood as well. When I penned this chapter, "The Dance with the Devil," I had returned from a mission trip to Haiti. Before I left for my trip, my son-in-law, Mike, asked me how I was coming along in writing my book. I told him I was waiting to return from Haiti to finish a chapter called "The Dance with the Devil." He replied, "So you think you will experience that in Haiti?" I said, "Yes," but I could have never imagined to what degree.

My journey to Haiti was one I will never forget. The images in my mind of the destitution and devastation are beyond words; the looks in the faces of the hopeless, the debris from the 2010 Earthquake, scattered people looking for food, water and help. It was so overwhelming! I wouldn't know where to start even if I had all the money in the world.

A team of seven people from our church, a missionary, the late Cindy Zimmerman, and another girl, Cara, from Lancaster, PA, came together to share whatever little we could offer the people of Haiti. We fed and clothed orphans; we visited the sick mommas and babies at the hospital; we scheduled a movie night in the mountains for the community - we showed the "Chronicles of Narnia" in French (Haitians speak French Creole); we fed the community a meal; we visited two schools; we danced together; we did a craft with many children and the list goes on. More than what we could do for them was what they did for us.

People there who are Christians are genuinely happy and thank God for all things. They love God. They worship Him from the wee hours of the morning through the late evening. We stayed with a family who would leave the radio on all night with worship songs in English. The radio was rigged with wire and attached to a pole that was attached to a tree. How they got reception is beyond me!

I had the privilege to share dance with the Haitian children by bringing 12 pairs of tap shoes with me that I thought they might enjoy. When I opened my tap bag after a large community gathering and said, "Come and get the tap shoes," women of all ages ran to the front where I was standing. I had the interpreter tell the ladies, "Piti-piti" (which means small). I felt overwhelmed and was sorry that we had to turn these ladies and children away. Many women returned to their seats with sad expressions. I wished I had tap shoes for all.

The children were scrambling to see if the shoes fit so they could get up and show off their new tap shoes! Twelve girls found shoes that fit! After the shoes were on, I began to teach them very basic steps. The sounds made on the concrete floor from the shoes amazed them. They giggled and had a grand old time. The tap shoes did not leave their feet for the duration of my visit in that mountain area. They wore those shoes to school, church and everywhere. I didn't know if it was because they didn't have any shoes or simply because they liked the clicking-clacking so much.

After the young girls sat down, I welcomed the ladies of all ages to come up front. There must have been 60 women stuffed in the school/church/community center. I taught them tap steps and they, too, giggled in amazement, like the little girls, over the shoes that made sounds while they watched my feet and imitated the dance steps. How a simple little thing like tap changed our way of communication! Dance is a universal language and we were able to laugh, have fun and, for a short time, take their minds off the troubles that were so evident in all their lives. God was using my feet like in the Leeland song! The mountains of Charrier will never be the same since tap has been introduced! Fun! Fun! Fun! Dance Party! I can't wait to see what Heaven will be like! Will we be able to have tap shoes while praising Jesus? I do not know. But we had a little bit of the joy of heaven on earth while in Charrier!

Here is the article written in a missions update by Cindy Zimmerman, the missionary to Haiti, about our team in the mountains Charrier.

"Seven members from Agape Fellowship Church spent a week in Haiti.
They spent time at the school in Charrier teaching a class on abstinence.

They provided a meal for the Charrier school as well as one for Dina's orphanage in Montrouis. The highlight was tap dancing. Cheryl Smith is a tap-dancing instructor. When she brought out those tap shoes the kids just had a blast. With music being such an important part of the Haitian culture, tap dancing became an instant hit. The boys playing the drums had a great time. Everyone got involved. What a great ministry. Who would have ever thought? Never underestimate your gifts how they may bless others."

I also had the opportunity to share the message of abstinence with the students from the Christian school and the community. I was not sure how this would go over. Most of these families live in one room; they see each other physically changing all the time and are most likely introduced to seeing or having sex at a young age due to the culture.

At one point in my message to the community I felt inspired to share about God's love to them. I told them the illustration of how when I was dating my boyfriend and he was leaving to go home, I came up with a symbol that I could use to say I love you without saying a word. I would lift my right hand and use the three middle fingers and tuck my pinky and thumb inside. This symbol meant "1-2-3, I LOVE YOU!" So, whenever my boyfriend left, I would show the three fingers. I never had to say a word yet he knew what I was saying. That boyfriend is now my husband, Gary. When our children were old enough to understand, I would use my right hand and put up three fingers to tell them "1-2-3, I LOVE YOU" when they were at the bus stop, riding away from home with friends, at school in their classroom or playing with friends! I carry on the tradition with grandchildren too! I told the people of Charrier, "Let's tell God '1-2-3, We Love Him!" We all placed our hand up with three fingers and told God, "1-2-3, I LOVE YOU!" Then I told them I wanted them to know, from me, "1-2-3, I LOVE YOU" and I held up three fingers to them. "Now, when you see me somewhere, hold up three fingers to me and I will know '1-2-3, YOU LOVE ME!'" To my surprise, as we walked and rode around Charrier, children, moms, young boys and people who were not even at the gathering would hold up three fingers to tell our team that they loved us! How the word spread quickly! How powerful three fingers can be! Thank God for this simple, little illustration that helped us with another bridge to the communication gap!

"Blessed is he who considers the poor;
The LORD will deliver him in time of trouble.
The LORD will preserve him and keep him alive,
And he will be blessed on the earth;
You will not deliver him to the will of his enemies.
The LORD will strengthen him on his bed of illness;
You will sustain him on his sickbed."
Psalm 41:1-3

The next section may be the most misunderstood part you will read. It may cause you to doubt my experience or question what the truth is from what I share. Please know that I tell you the truth and have witnesses to confirm what I went through in Haiti. I believe this was my life verse for Haiti as well as for my return home!

The part of my trip that deals with "The Dance with the Devil" was foreign to me and many of my team members. So much so, at times I thought I might be losing my mind. Knowing I was going to Haiti, and understanding that Voodoo is the national religion, I asked many to pray for me. What happened was very disconcerting and unnerving. I struggled to pen what took place, because I really did not want to relive what happened.

We left for our trip from the States on Friday, October 28, and arrived in Charrier, Haiti, after a long ride in the back of a dump truck. We took a three-hour ride through Port-au-Prince where the streets are filled with people begging for money, United Nation workers with machine guns here and there, and people scattered everywhere just walking the streets with no direction. The chocolate-colored river was filled with people doing their laundry, bathing and cooling off. The river didn't seem fit for animals even though they, too, were in the water. The ride up the mountains was filled with different smells that I had never inhaled before. I couldn't figure out whether it was trash being burned or just the heat radiating off the dry, parched ground. Later, I was told it was what they call charcoal that they burn to help them cook their meals.

When we arrived at our destination, I was taken back a bit. Even though we had photos to see where we would be staying, the place was lined and protected by cactus and a gate that was falling off the hinges with a chain linked around it. Cactus for our protection – a gate falling down that could be kicked over? Wow - this WAS going to take faith!

I mentioned in an earlier chapter that I had never camped before in my life other than a family trip when I was a young girl in a motorhome with all the meals made prior to the trip. Not really camping! So, to sleep in a tent (on an air mattress - yeah), use a concrete hole in the ground to go to the bathroom and wash with buckets of cold water was definitely camping! I am so proud I was able to overcome those obstacles and didn't complain about them once while I was there! That is God!

The first couple of nights I struggled just to find rest in a new and different surrounding camping in the mountains in a tent - hoping not to see any scorpions, rats or snakes! Even so, I must say it was beautiful and peaceful with the chickens, goats, kittens and roosters surrounding our tents. Just very noisy!

I asked our interpreter, Alage, about October 31 - if Haitian's celebrate Halloween. He did not know what Halloween was, so I assumed it is just an American cultural celebration. I felt at ease thinking that maybe there would not be the intense spiritual warfare for which I *thought* I had prepared ahead of time.

During the night of Tuesday, November 1, I was awakened by the sounds of drums. Immediately, I had no peace. I was told a witchdoctor lived across the dirt road a couple houses down. I slept in the tent with Cindy the missionary and Cara from another church. No one else seemed to be awake. I couldn't understand why no one was coming out of their tent to see what these drum sounds were? Everyone seemed to remain restful, snoring and asleep.

As I lie awake, I remembered this night was November 1st, which is All Saint's Day, and thought maybe this was what they were celebrating. I could hear screams and a conch-shell call along with the drums. It seemed to me to be getting louder and louder. I was waiting for people in their tents to get up and congregate outside, because I was sure everyone else could hear it, also. I lie on my air mattress praying but becoming very fearful. I shook and could not control my anxiety. I prayed everything I knew to pray. I felt like God was so far away; as far away as my family was from me in the States. I knew this was a lie from the devil, but it was pounding in my mind so powerfully! Where was He when I needed Him most some thousands of miles away from home and family?

I began to suit myself up with God's spiritual armor as Ephesians 6 tells us we should do: the helmet of salvation, the breastplate of righteousness, girding my waist with truth, the gospel sandals, the shield of faith and the sword of the Spirit - I quoted over and over again. I tried so hard to get back to sleep but sleep evaded me. Cindy was tossing about on her air mattress in the middle of the night so I asked her if she would pray for me, which she did. We talked about the drums and she tried to console me. By morning when Cara awoke, I asked her if she heard the drums. She didn't. Why did I hear them? I did not want to hear them! I was so out of sorts by morning that after Cara and Cindy were dressed for the day and left the tent, I lay prostrate, face down on an air mattress and cried out to God, "What was that all about last night? Why did I feel like You were not with me?" I tried to pause and hear from God. I said I put on the suit of armor and I still did not feel protected. I felt as if God showed me through His Word and in my mind that there was a *crack in my armor*. What does that mean; a crack in my armor? I pondered this and I read back through the warfare chapter in the Book of Ephesians.

"Finally, my brethren, be strong in the Lord and in the power of His might. Put on the whole armor of God, that you may be able to stand against the wiles of the devil. For we do not wrestle against flesh and blood, but against principalities, against powers, against the rulers of the darkness of this age, against spiritual hosts of wickedness in the heavenly places. Therefore, take up the whole armor of God, that you may be able to withstand in the evil day, and having done all, to stand. Stand therefore, having girded your waist with truth, having put on the breastplate of righteousness, and having shod your feet with the preparation of the gospel of peace; above all, taking the shield of faith with which, you will be able to quench all the fiery darts of the wicked one. And take the helmet of salvation, and the sword of the Spirit, which is the word of God; praying always with all prayer and supplication in the Spirit, being watchful to this end with all perseverance and supplication for all the saints and for me, that utterance may be given to me, that I may open my mouth boldly to make known the mystery of the gospel, for which I am an ambassador in chains; that in it I may speak boldly, as I ought to speak."
(Ephesians 6:10-20)

The words *stand, withstand and stand therefore*, came through to me like darts. You do not want to stand; you do not want this battle. You want to close your eyes and ears to what is happening. You betcha I did! When trying to sleep, I even put on an eye mask to see no evil and ear plugs to hear no evil! But that made it even louder as the earplugs intensified the drum sounds and of my heart beating faster and faster. But God was calling me to *stand*! He just spoke to my heart, "You stand and I will fight the battle. This is not your battle, but Mine!" Oh my! What was I to do with that? Okay, so as we met for morning devotions everyone came together and they were rested and did not hear the drums. They prayed for me to rest and remember that *greater* is He (God) than he (Satan - little god) that is in the world (I John 4:4). So, God gave me the grace that day to make it through that sleepless dance.

That next night, Tuesday into Wednesday, as I lay down to go to sleep, I prayed and asked God to help me with my spiritual suit of armor and help me to *stand*. This night was even worse than the first night. As I tried to comfort myself with songs and hymns and spiritual songs against the loud sounds of the drums that seemed to get closer and closer, I was intensely unsettled! I prayed but woke Cindy up and asked her to pray with me. I even needed to go to the bathroom but was afraid to leave the tent. Cindy went to the bathroom with me and told me she thought the ceremony was way off in the distance. When I was in the tent, the sounds were so loud to me. Even with the earplugs in, my heart and ears pounded with the drums so thunderously that I could not rest. I felt as if I was actually in their ceremony. I know this is strange to say, but I was being told by Satan: *You are mine! You are on my ground! You will not be going home! This is it!*

In the night while everyone else was sleeping and each hour felt like an eternity, you can think of so many strange thoughts. I was remembering back to when my husband was a pastor in Cambridge, Maryland. They had animal sacrifices in that area. Someone once told me that Satan worshipers want to have the purest sacrifices: pastors, pastor's wives or the pastor's children. My heart was pounding so intensely. Why did I ever need to know that? Was I to be their sacrifice? They knew I was there and my testimony was making a difference in Charrier with dance and abstinence. My fear was so great that I wanted to run, but had nowhere to go. I felt like a caged animal. For hours this took place! I finally fell asleep in the wee hours of the morning.

The drums continued from 10 p.m. to 5 a.m. in the morning. Alage, the interpreter, told us that we were in the height of the Voodoo celebration that kicks off on All Saints' Day and lasts for several nights. Oh, my word! How was I going to make it another night? I had victory during the day and to my amazement and others, despite my shortage of sleep, God gave me super strength to dance and lead people every time we gathered. Having a *dance party* was a given each day and night!

Wednesday we left the mountains of Charrier and moved two and a half hours down the coastline to Montrouis, a beach-front mission home. I was hopeful that perhaps, now, I will have left the sleepless nights in the mountains. The mission home had a bedroom supplied with six beds for all the ladies to be in one room together with a bathroom attached. I was looking forward to a good night's sleep on a real bed (Air mattresses are nice but when they deflate, you spend all night trying to hold your body up). Forgive me for complaining, since native Momma (our hostess in the mountains), slept on the dirt floor at night to cool off so her guests had the best accommodations.

Wednesday into Thursday morning sleeping proved to be another night when everyone rested except me. Several hours after trying to sleep I decided to get my flashlight and see what time it was. I was not surprised; it was 3am. Why do I say that? Satanist's ceremonies end and call up the spirits before 3am. I didn't fall asleep until after 4am, because before we went to bed the drums in this area started at 9pm.

When I was lying in bed praying for others, my family and asking God to wake up people in the United States to pray for me, a team member from our church got up to go the bathroom. Since I was awake and could not sleep because the drums seemed even louder at Montrouis than in the mountains, I assumed she was restless and could not sleep as well. I asked her if she was ok. She said, "Yes, why"? I responded, "Because of the drums." She replied, "I can't hear any drums." I urged, "Come to the window. You can hear them *now*, can't you?" She replied, "I really don't hear anything." We were both puzzled. Why was I hearing the drums and she wasn't? I went back to the bed and lay there saying, "God, am I just hearing things? Why are they so loud to me but not the others?" I finally fell asleep clutching my Bible.

In the morning at breakfast, I was so glad to hear some of the men on the trip ask me if I heard the drums last night. Was I ever relieved! So, I wasn't going crazy! Judi asked one of the local Christian men, who was our driver the next day, why she could not hear the drums but I could. He replied that God wanted me to hear them. Not sure at that point why that was and still do not know to the fullest unless it was for the penning of this chapter.

The next night was the worst of all. I had, by now, learned that for every Voodoo group celebrating and worshiping Satan, there are Christians praying, praising and worshiping God at the same time. I thought this fact would bring me more comfort as I tried to sleep. Thursday night into Friday morning heavy drums began pounding even louder than before. I tried the earplugs but the noise intensified. I could not shut it out.

As I laid in bed praying, reciting scripture and singing songs, I think I finally dosed off, but not for long. I woke to a full sweat and sat straight up in bed as if someone had pushed me up from my sleeping position. The drums proceeded to get louder and louder. I was told by the enemy: *I am coming for you and you will not return home!* I felt as if the enemy further said: *You want to Dance with me? I will show you what that looks like!* I felt like there was a tug of war for my life, not my soul, because Satan could do nothing to my soul because I am the Lord's child. I could not take it any longer! I whispered in the quiet room where five other ladies slept soundly, "Cindy. Cindy." Louder; "Cindy." And one final louder; "Cindy!" She woke up. She asked if I was okay. I said, "No!" I shook uncontrollably and was sweating. I began to hyperventilate. She came over and began to pray over me as well as two other ladies who were awakened. The other two ladies, Cara and Sandy, slept through the whole ordeal. And, the reason why? Probably because the next night they were awake throwing up all night. They needed the calm before their storm. Eventually, I calmed down and fell asleep.

The next morning at devotions I sensed that the team may be tired of or perplexed as to why I was going through this situation. I felt like Job, when Zophar, Bildad and Eliphaz were trying to counsel him about why he was going through his health issues and the losses of his family, finances and livestock. I felt very misunderstood. I walked around in a quandary.

So, now it is Friday and I can't wait to go home to see my family! I am saying, "God get me through one more night and I will be home free!" Friday night descended with the drums starting at 9pm and ongoing throughout the night, but this night was different. My friends, Sandy and Cara, were so sick that the mission home had to keep the generator on all night so they could go to the bathroom and be able to see where they were going. Usually by 10pm the government in Haiti turns the electric off, but on this last night the lights were on outside and inside the building. It rained for a while, so I rested better seeing lights outside and hearing the rain. On that last night I could actually hear the worship music by a church group over the sound of the drums. Perhaps God was making it possible for me to concentrate on His music, not the enemy's!

PAUSE

Recently, after reading Facing Terror, the true story of missionaries, Carrie McDonnall and her husband, David, who paid the ultimate price for his love of the Muslim people, I was smitten by something that happened to Carrie after she survived a terrorist attack in Iraq. David did not survive the attack. As Carrie was healing in a Texas hospital from all the wounds she sustained, she began to hear singing. Here is an excerpt.

"One night as I lay in bed, I began hearing the sound of men's voices singing; like an old-time choir. I thought, at first, it must be coming from an adjoining hospital room. They sang beautifully. The sound of their voices relaxed me and the conviction with which they sang encouraged me.
My mother was already asleep on her cot and I knew she was tired, but I so wanted her to hear this beautiful music. I thought she might go to the room next door and ask them to come to my room, or at least tell them how much I was enjoying listening to them. I called to my mother and asked her if she could hear the singing. "No, baby," she said.
I listened more closely to the words: "Lord, we thank You for the cross, we thank You for our lives . . . Lord, we praise You with our hearts." I thought, "Wow, this is a group that can sing!" I want them in my room, Mama," I said. "Mama, can you hear it?" "No, I don't hear it," Mom said. "Are you sure? I know I am not going crazy! I'm not!" I then told her the words of the song and where it was coming from.
My mom got up and put her head against the wall. "No, I don't hear it, baby. I'm sorry." "Well, me, too," I told her. "You're missing out." "Well, enjoy it, baby." She climbed back onto her bed and said, "Maybe it's the Lord allowing this to be sung over you. Relax and enjoy it."

This portion of Carrie's story brought me much peace. It helped me to understand that there are times when not everyone is able to hear what God wants another person to hear. At times, God chooses to allow some people a brief encounter into the spiritual realm, which others are not permitted to experience, for whatever His reason. I am thankful I finally heard the singing of the saints over the chants of the wicked.

In the middle of the night I was praying for everyone who was sick; Sandy, Cara and a guy named Andy. I couldn't sleep well because of the three people sick, but was thrilled to be going home the next day! While lying in my bed on my stomach I was looking out at the Caribbean Sea, hearing the waves and thanking God for the lights that seemed to comfort me. I felt as I was praying that God spoke, *"These lights are for your protection."* I didn't wish sickness on anyone, but because they were violently throwing up, the lights were provided during their sickness – and I was thankful for the lights! The next day we were heading home and I was thrilled! I made it through the storm!

16
The Bitter & Sweet
Dance Home

When I arrived home in York, Pennsylvania, I literally kissed the ground after kissing my husband! It was the best blessing to be home! The next day I was thrilled to be singing at our church with the whole family and excited to be back on American soil with a greater appreciation for a husband to hold, family, hot water, food, a wonderful bed, clothing and too much more to list.

During the worship set, I sang like they sang in Haiti. Boy, can they sing -- long and heartfelt singing -- not just going through the motions or mouthing words! During the service many of our team members gave testimony of what God did in Haiti and in us. I stood and gave praise to God for returning home to my family and church. I truly didn't think I was coming home after all the lies the enemy shot at me. Remember Satan said: *You are mine. You are on my ground. You are not leaving here!* To which I argued, *"I am **not** yours, I **am** on God's ground; He owns it all. I **am** going home!"*

Monday morning after a restless night's sleep, it felt like a chemistry set was bubbling in my stomach. My first thought was I was coming down with what the other team members had the night before we left. I thought I was home free from any illness. After many hours of tossing and turning I began to hit the commode. Thank God it only flowed from my lower end and not both like the team members experienced. After about fifteen trips to the commode, I couldn't leave the bathroom. I felt so nauseated that I thought I would vomit, also. I heard my son, Josh, get up for work and told him to grab me a bucket in case I couldn't get up. I was so weak. As soon as he returned with the bucket, I asked him to get his dad, because I felt as if I was going to pass out. Gary was not supposed to be home that morning, but God kept him home for me. *Thank you, Lord!* Gary put a cold rag to my head and held my head in his hands. I couldn't even hold my head up. From the top of my head to my lower extremities I had a strange feeling as if my life's blood was leaving my body. At that time, my husband tells me, I passed out.

He heard me groan for a couple seconds in a voice he had never heard before. He described it as if it were demonic. He said it sounded like something was leaving my body. He looked at me and saw my hands clenched and curled upward and my head dropped to the side with what he called the Death Stare. From all of his pastoral experience, he said he had only seen that look in people he has witnessed who had died. He tried to detect my pulse but couldn't feel anything. He panicked in his heart and said to God, "You brought her back from Haiti and now this? Please God don't let it end this way!" About 20 seconds later I said to him, "I think I'm going to pass out." He replied, "You just did." I told him at that point I thought he should get an ambulance to take me to the hospital, since I was in no condition to get up and would have to be carried out. He called 911 and the ambulance arrived shortly.

Upon coming into the bathroom and finding out I had just returned from Haiti, the EMTs immediately placed masks on their faces. This was before the Covid Pandemic, so it was very scary. I was really concerned at that point not knowing what I had contracted. I was thinking they thought it was Cholera or some other foreign disease. Not sure how to get me from the commode to the stretcher, my husband wanted me to be covered, for my sake, at least with my underwear. There are times when you don't care at all what you look like or what you are wearing – this was one of those. I ended up in my t-shirt and panties. It didn't matter to me what anyone saw at that point; I just needed to get better. I clung and hung onto Josh, 21 at the time, who led the way out of the bathroom and down the hallway, because the stretcher would not be able to be turned down the hallway into the bedroom. My husband held me up from behind. So, making my entrance onto the stretcher at the bottom of my outside steps in my underwear and t-shirt was not an issue to me. Only two neighbors were outside; thank God! As they strapped me down on the stretcher and wrapped me up, I thought, I don't even feel as if I am in my own body. You know, I have to say this for all those who do not know me; I am as Evangelical as they come. I walk the straight-and-narrow way and hold to sound Biblical doctrine, but all of this successfully broke my mold. From what I experienced, this was stepping way outside the box for me.

After the EMTs whisked me away to the hospital, Josh went back through our bedroom to clean the bathroom. Thank you, Josh! He later related that when he entered the room, he thought he saw a black shadow dash into the bathroom. At first, he thought maybe someone was still in the house, but after going back into the bathroom with the light on, he wondered what it could have been. He went about cleaning the bathroom and after briefly leaving the room he returned and saw the same black shadow again. Josh thought it was odd and realized our dog, Bailey, was downstairs and not upstairs with him. Bailey always wants to be around people, but she apparently sensed something was not right. Josh said, when he thought about it, the shadow looked like the souvenirs I brought back from Haiti which were hand-carved in soapstone by the Haitian people.

So, back to the scene with the ambulance where I was barely conscious. Nevertheless, I overheard that my temperature was 94 degrees. I am not a nurse but I knew that was really low. The funny thing is, I never really experienced any pain through all of this, just nausea and discomfort, which was not as bad as some flus or viruses I've had. I must have gone into extreme dehydration because they had to stick me three times to successfully secure a needle in my arm to start an IV.

The EMTs were talking to me and asking lots of questions. I can only remember a little of what was happening. I just wanted to sleep. As we approached the hospital, I knew my husband and son were trying to scramble to call family, friends and church members to pray. I really did feel as if I was on the wings of an angel and God's 'amazing grace' enveloped me. As soon as I was pushed into the hospital, they rolled me into a room labeled 'Quarantine.' I was in isolation and everyone who entered had to wear a mask. I began to feel so alone and shut off until I saw my husband.

After we talked awhile, Gary made his way to the hospital waiting room where many church people had come to pray once they got word of my sickness. I was so touched by their love and concern, but couldn't yet tell them how much I appreciated all they were doing!

My sister, Tanya, the head guidance counselor at a high school in Reisterstown, Maryland, was at work and left her job to pick up my mom some 30 minutes away and continued to drive her to the hospital in York, Pennsylvania, which was an additional 45-minute drive. When they arrived at the hospital, my mom came into the room with me and the doctor came in to say they were thinking I was going to need a blood transfusion because they thought I was losing blood even though they did not see any blood. The doctors proceeded to tell me that if I had to get blood that there was a chance that my throat could close up and, if so, I would need a tracheotomy. I know they had to give me the rundown but . . . what in the world? My mom's face paled as white as snow, and I just wanted to cry. All I kept saying was, "Lord, I don't want anyone else's blood; nothing but the blood of Jesus! E. Coli was a potential diagnosis, also. I told Gary to go to the waiting room and ask the people to pray that I would not need blood. Somehow word got out all over York County and many people, including several friends who were pastor's wives, went to give blood in my name at the blood bank just in case it was needed. Wow! How touching!

Thank God, with many of God's people praying from York, to California, to Africa, to New York and beyond, God wonderfully raised me up following several hours of IV fluids. I never needed medication or a blood transfusion. *All to the glory of God!* I was released from the hospital the next day, Wednesday, and returned home. I immediately took all the souvenirs from the house and disposed of them in the garage. Even though my friend and I prayed and anointed every item before we brought it home, I still felt the need to get rid of them.

At the beginning, after answering the call to go to Haiti for a mission trip in October, my parents were very concerned about me going and expressed that they didn't want me to go on the trip. After much prayer I still believed I was to go on the trip. Before leaving for Haiti, I gathered my family together, including my mom and dad. I wanted them to know that if anything were to happen to me, I would be in Heaven. I told my family that I would want to see them there as well. My words must have replayed often in my dad's mind while I was away in Haiti.

So, the Wednesday that I came home from the hospital and while I was resting from the accumulated trauma abroad and sickness I experienced at home, I was about to receive an early 2011 Christmas present – my Christmas miracle! My dad, who lives in Maryland, came to Pennsylvania to visit me. He and I were alone at that time, so we talked without any interruptions. Dad began by sharing things that were on his heart. My dad needed to tell me that he was going back to his beginnings; his roots. This was his way of telling me that he was seeking God. Was I hearing this right? After 26 years of prayer, was I witnessing God at work once again and this time with my dad? Well, to shorten what took place, I had the awesome opportunity to kneel beside my dad and pray the sinner's prayer with him while he asked Christ to come into his life with tears streaming down his 75-year-old face. What a miracle -- the rebirth of a person, my daddy! What an early Christmas gift for me and my family!

God is so good! Remember Romans 8:28? My Haiti trip, my illness and all that I was going through, God turned around and used it to draw my dad near to him! Praise God! Despite the things I endured, it was worth it all. My dad began reading the Bible I gave him and my husband and I discipled him. There again – "Nothing but the Blood of Jesus" – what Jesus did on the cross for us!

For our Thanksgiving service at Agape Fellowship church, we would celebrate our thankful praises to God by setting up a barren tree that gets filled with the praises of God's people by placing apple ornaments on the tree; each apple representing a thanksgiving, as I previously described in our pastorate in Cambridge, Maryland. This was a tradition started by our former pastor, Charles Jennings, at our home church in Baltimore, Maryland, which we adopted and practiced in every church Gary has pastored. At the end of the service the tree is filled with the fruit of *praises* to God. My praise was about my dad receiving Christ after praying for him for 26 years. I referred to the scripture verse in Luke 18, the parable of the Woman and the Judge.

> *"Then He spoke a parable to them, that men always ought to pray and not lose heart, saying: 'There was in a certain city a judge who did not fear God nor regard man. Now there was a widow in that city; and she came to him saying, 'Get justice for me from my adversary.' And he would not for a while; but afterward he said within himself, 'Though I do not fear God nor regard man, yet because this widow troubles me I will avenge her, lest by her continual coming she weary me.' Then the Lord said, 'Hear what the unjust judge said. And shall God not avenge His own elect who cry out day and night to Him, though He bears long with them? I tell you that He will avenge them speedily. Nevertheless, when the Son of Man comes, will He really find faith on the earth?'"*
> *(Luke 18:1-8)*

I believe that God answers our prayers His way and in His time. I challenged the people of our church, Agape Fellowship, to *not lose heart*; continue to pray for your loved ones for salvation. I can come to God and petition Him, troubling Him, so to speak, again and again, so He will say, "I will grant her the answer she is praying for." The illustration of the woman making the judge weary as John MacArthur writes in a footnote:

> *". . . she weary me: literally means, 'hit under the eye in the Greek." What the judge would not do out of compassion for the widow or reverence for God, he would do out of sheer frustration with her incessant pleading." (The MacArthur Study Bible, p 1551, Footnote Luke 18)*

John MacArthur also comments:

> *". . . listen to the point of the story, namely, that God, who always does right and is filled with compassion for believers who suffer, will certainly respond to His beloved ones who cry out for His help. Speedily: He may delay long, but He does so for a good reason . . . and when He acts, His vengeance is swift." (The MacArthur Study Bible, p. 1551, Footnotes Luke 18:6, 8)*

God answered my prayers His way and, in His time, and used what I was going through to draw my dad to Himself. Stay encouraged. Remain in prayer for your lost loved ones who need Christ or have strayed away from Him! Remember the only thing we can take to Heaven is another human soul! God help us to keep our eyes on that prize.

Since I have had time to process my trip to Haiti and really reflect on what happened, I was led to these scripture verses.

"Inasmuch then as the children have partaken of flesh and blood, He Himself likewise shared in the same, that through death He might destroy him who had the power of death, that is, the devil, and release those who through fear of death were all their lifetime subject to bondage." (Hebrews 2:14-15).

Here again, John MacArthur writes in his footnote (The MacArthur Study Bible, p. 1900, Footnote Hebrews 2:14):

"Jesus came to earth to die. By dying, He was able to conquer death in His resurrection. By conquering death, He rendered Satan powerless against all who are saved. [Yippee! – My addition] Satan's using the power of death is subject to God's will." (Job 2:6)

MacArthur's footnote – Fear of Death (The MacArthur Study Bible, p. 1900, Footnote Hebrews 2:15):

"For the believer, 'death is swallowed up in victory.' Therefore, the fear of death and its spiritual bondage has been brought to an end through the works of Christ."

I believe with all of my heart that there was a tug-of-war for my life while I was in Haiti; not for my soul because that belongs to God. I believe that Satan was battling for my physical life and God said: *She is Mine and it is not her time!* Some may be skeptical and query: Can there actually be something like this *for real* out there? All I can tell you is, experiencing firsthand the spiritual attack and warfare I battled in Haiti and upon my return home, I am so very thankful for my life! There will be other *Dances with the Devil* as long as I have breath, but I hope I am better prepared for them after my experiences in Haiti.

"I HOPE YOU DANCE"
Mark D. Sanders and Tia Sillers

I hope you never lose your sense of wonder
You get your fill to eat but always keep that hunger
May you never take one single breath for granted
GOD forbid love ever leave you empty-handed
I hope you still feel small when you stand beside the ocean
Whenever one door closes I hope one more opens
Promise me that you'll give faith a fighting chance
And when you get the choice to sit it out or dance
I hope you dance .... I hope you dance

17
My Haiti Tug-of-War
- A Psalm of Severe Struggle

A large number of the Psalms written by King David centered around struggles and dangers he faced. He was honest with God and cried out for help, keeping his faith in his God whom he knew would rescue him somehow. Just because he fully believed in God did not mean that he was above struggling with difficult emotions, because he did. And he spelled out to God his honest words of how he was feeling during those grueling times. But he kept his focus on the God he knew. Even at times when he got down pretty low, he still chose to believe God, trusting that God was going to rescue him.

So that you may understand the emotional, mental and spiritual struggles I endured on my mission trip to Haiti, I kept a journal documenting the fierce encounters with spiritual warfare as well as the blessings of what God did in Haiti. I will always remember. Like King David, these are my Haiti Psalms.

Sunday Morning - October 30, 2011

Thank you, Lord, for a good night's sleep! Praise You! Lord, yesterday was amazing. The lesson prepared was abandoned! We had women, children and men. You changed my message to salvation, suit of armor and love of God. I think God blessed. The heart-shaped love symbol and the 1-2-3 hand symbol broke through the barrier. Then the best - tap shoes for the children. They learned some tap steps. Then Alage (my interpreter) offered for the women to come up. There were about 60 women. We all danced together. It was great! God, You are Amazing! Father, the people love You and praise You all day long! No complaining! This is a church day. I can't wait.

Sunday Evening - October 30, 2011

God, please bring some heat relief. It is so hot! Thank You for a good night's sleep. You have refreshed me. Church was interesting. The people love to sing with all their hearts. God, You are beautiful! I bless You! These people seem to have such a love for You and love to worship You. I am amazed. You have helped me each day with my anxiety. I have enjoyed dancing with the children, women, and people at Momma's home. Today, we saw a rainbow from the storm that cooled us off. Another reminder You are here with us.

October 31, 2011

Lord, today I have been overwhelmed with anxiety. I broke down and cried. God, give me Your peace. God, give me Your words today. Father, show me what to say. I need You! Lord, thank You for yesterday. I was able to teach at the school - maybe 70 students. I gave my testimony and talked to them about abstinence. Then later we had a session for adults in the afternoon. In the evening we had a movie, "Chronicles of Narnia" in French for the community to watch. It was so cool to see the people come out and stand for a two-hour movie. Would we do that in the States? No, we need the latest and greatest!

November 1, 2011

Thank You, Lord, that it is morning. God, last night was the worst. I wanted to sleep but the Voodoo drums were so loud. So loud! I had earplugs in and it sounded like it was close by. Oh God, I shook so badly that Cindy climbed into my bed and held me. We prayed. We went to the bathroom and heard the drums were far away. Not close - that helped. I still did not go back to sleep until much later. Oh, God, why did You want me to hear that so loud? I am not sure what the meaning is? God, I pray You give me rest tonight.

As I prayed in the morning for the suit of armor, I sensed that God was saying, "There is a crack in your armor." What does that mean? I do not understand. God, I need to see what needs to be shored-up. I thank You for a wonderful time in Charrier. The people welcomed us and the children had such a wonderful time dancing unto the Lord. I bless You. They have so little and know You so well. We have so much and know You so little! We took a three-hour ride from Charrier, the mountains, to Montrouis, the beach. We are now at the Life Connection mission Home. We have single beds and a nice room. The waterfront beach is absolutely beautiful. You are amazing, from the mountains to the Caribbean. Father, be with us the rest of the trip. Keep us safe. Provide a time of rest today. I bless You. God, I miss my family. I need You to help me. God, would You give my parents peace knowing each day is a day closer to me coming home. Bless Your Name!

November 2, 2011

Lord, today is a new day! Joy comes in the morning. Last night, I slept from 8pm till 2am. I was awakened by the drums and could not go back to sleep. God calmed me down and then I was able to pray. My friend got up to go to the bathroom. I asked her if she could hear the drums. She could not. I believe God showed me that I am to pray. I think the "crack in the armor" is that I am to stand - not fall down, retreat or avoid the battle. I can only stand in the might of God.

Lord, it seems surreal that yesterday I was in the mountains of Haiti tapping with the children. Lord, I pray for today. Not sleeping too well last night, I need You once again to give me strength. I need You! Lord, be with Gary back home and my family. I miss them all so badly! Sometimes I cry when no one else is around. I bless You! I believe I will be safe to return to York Saturday!

November 4, 2011

Today is the last day before we leave. I praise You for Your watch and care! You are my strong tower.

November 8, 2011

Thank You, Lord, I made it safe out of Haiti. You kept me! I know it was only You! God, You spared me. I thank You for bringing me back to the States before I got sick. Lord, yesterday when Gary held my head, I passed out; he thought I had died. I was out for about 20 seconds. He saw the death stare and thought I had died. Thank You, Lord, You saved me.

Always remember when you are going through great struggles, you are not alone. As Christians, we are all in a very real spiritual war. And we're in this together. As the Apostle Paul has revealed to us in the Scriptures, we are in a war that, although it is spiritual, we experience it in the physical world.

> " A final word: Be strong in the Lord and in His mighty power. Put on all of God's armor so that you will be able to stand firm against all strategies of the devil. For we are not fighting against flesh-and-blood enemies, but against evil rulers and authorities of the unseen world, against mighty powers in this dark world, and against evil spirits in the heavenly places.
> Therefore, put on every piece of God's armor so you will be able to resist the enemy in the time of evil. Then after the battle you will still be standing firm. Stand your ground, putting on the belt of truth and the body armor of God's righteousness. For shoes, put on the peace that comes from the Good News so that you will be fully prepared. In addition to all of these, hold up the shield of faith to stop the fiery arrows of the devil. Put on salvation as your helmet, and take the sword of the Spirit, which is the word of God." (Ephesians 6:10-17)

And through the help of the Holy Spirit, and by our wise compliance with the Word of God, we stand our ground -- WE OVERCOME THE BATTLE!

18
One Ministries

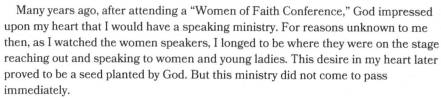

Many years ago, after attending a "Women of Faith Conference," God impressed upon my heart that I would have a speaking ministry. For reasons unknown to me then, as I watched the women speakers, I longed to be where they were on the stage reaching out and speaking to women and young ladies. This desire in my heart later proved to be a seed planted by God. But this ministry did not come to pass immediately.

God thrust me into a speaking ministry after several years of teaching and developing a Women's Ministry by attending Elmbrook Church for three years in Wisconsin with many other women from our church. After being equipped by this ministry, the Lord prompted me to motivate and mentor women in Christ through Bible study and leadership training. This launched many opportunities to speak at churches, youth groups and a Bible college. "Truth in Love" was developed as a speaking ministry and my main audience was women and youth.

> *"Those who are wise will shine like the bright heavens. And those who lead many to do what is right and good will shine like the stars forever and ever."*
> *(Daniel 12:3)*

During God's process of establishing the speaking ministry, I applied to a local crisis pregnancy center as an educator to go into public schools to share about STD's (sexually transmitted diseases) and their consequences. I didn't know how I was going to capture the hearts of young people to be willing to listen to an outsider coming into their classroom territory teaching about such a personal topic. After introducing myself, I would share with the students why I was passionate about abstinence. It wasn't because I *was* abstinent, but because I *was not* abstinent before I got married and now have regrets! I would continue relating the reality that the decisions we make at a young age often have long-lasting consequences. I captured their hearts and minds when I shared my abortion story. They were more willing to listen to the rest of the lesson because I became vulnerable and handed them something deeply intimate about my own life.

The Abstinence Educator dance continued for four years in the public schools, and then the door shut. Or, should I say, it slammed shut! The funds for teaching in the public sector were stripped and no longer available. I was faithful to this God-appointed opportunity while the door was still open and I related to the words Jesus spoke to his disciples:

> *"I must work the works of Him that sent me, while it is day: the night cometh, when no man can work." (John 9:4)*

Therefore, I began to seek God and He pointed me in the direction of reaching young people attending church with the message of abstinence. I was resistant at first because working with churches, youth groups and home-school families can be more difficult than with secular society due to the sensitive subject matter of sex. The church should be the venue through which youth hear about the delicate subject matter of sex, but many leaders and parents fear what their youth will be taught. Therefore, the message is silent in many churches. Youth find out from their friends at the lunch table, on the bus, from their cell phones, liberal classrooms, television, YouTube, Facebook and other sites on the internet.

I sought the Lord as to what this direction would look like; how it would come to be. During this timeframe of pursuing the Lord for answers, I was asked by my chiropractor if I would come to her home and share about abstinence and purity from God's perspective with her daughter who would be attending high school in the fall. It was after our time together that God impressed upon my heart the need to reinforce God's perspective of abstinence prior to marriage in a broader scope. Being in ministry as a pastor's wife at the time, I remained well aware that the Christian community deals with these same issues as the secular realm. Christian families are confronted with premarital sex, unplanned pregnancies, and potential STI's (Sexually Transmitted Infections) as well.

It was for this reason I believed God had called me to *One Ministries*. "One" is an abstinence curriculum designed to reach and teach young people, middle school through college ages, about God's perspective on abstinence and the consequences of living a life outside of God's protective plan. It was tailored for churches, homeschool networks, colleges, Christian academies, public schools and individuals, addressing the ever-present danger of premarital sex that often leads to pregnancies and STI's and/or diseases.

I would speak to parents as well in my sessions. "One" has participated at Sandy Cove Conference Center in Northeast, Maryland, moderating a parent forum during a breakout session on the topic of "Open Conversation on Purity;" discussing how to share abstinence with your teen(s).

Having been an Abstinence Educator for four years trained through the "It's Smart to Wait" program, I had the privilege of teaching in the public middle and high schools, churches, Christian schools, Youth Groups, Women's Ministries and Lancaster Bible College. God continued to stoke my heart with passion to inform and enrich young people with the reasons why they should wait until their wedding night to have sex! It is God's plan and it is a wise and great plan by the designer of marriage! Sex is good. God invented it! My desire was to make a difference in young people's lives through "One Ministries!"

To help you understand a little more about me and "One," the following is a segment of an article published in the "Daily Record/Sunday News, York, PA, 2011" written by Melissa Nann Burke.

"At 17, Cheryl Smith was an aspiring professional dancer. She auditioned and was offered a spot with the Rockettes. She turned down the job to get married. But Smith didn't wait for her wedding night to have sex and that decision changed her life. 'I was not a Christian when I was dating or in the beginning of our marriage,' Smith said. 'When I saw God's plan, I asked Him to forgive me.'

Smith recalls the guilt and shame she felt, even though the man she slept with became her husband. After more than three decades, their marriage is still going strong (husband, Gary, heads the congregation at Agape Fellowship in York Township.)

Today, Smith speaks to groups of young people about abstinence – a practice she says is especially important in an era when premarital sex is so common. Surveys and public health data estimate anywhere from 85 percent to 95 percent of Americans have had premarital sex. Many of those did so by age 30."

The following is a snapshot of the purpose of One Ministries and my part in it as educator and speaker.

MY JOB
Abstinence Educator and Speaker

WHAT I DO: I have a ministry called One Ministries, which is an abstinence education program for middle school through high school-age youth. My message urges them to wait until marriage. I speak to them one-one-one or in group settings at churches, homes, organizations and schools. I share my personal testimony of my decision to have an abortion six months after I was married, and the cost of making decisions that have long-term consequences.

WHY I DO IT: I am passionate about the message of abstinence. I believe God has a plan for young people. If they know why God says... *wait until your wedding night,* then they might consider the benefits over the consequences before it is too late. I want them to know God has given us a chemical in our brains that's released when we engage in sexual activity. It bonds us to the person we are intimate with. Because of that, many people end up in a relationship with someone they had sex with, later separating, because all they had was this physical-sexual bond.

WHAT PEOPLE DON'T UNDERSTAND ABOUT MY WORK: The amount of time that's invested in starting a ministry from ground level – finances and other restrictions that keep you from doing what you believe so strongly in. I am a firm believer that abstinence should be taught to children from sixth grade through their college years.

SKILLS REQUIRED: I trained under the Worth the Wait program at Human Life Services. I also bring my personal testimony and 20-plus years in ministry, which included public speaking.

THREE JOBS I'VE HELD IN LIFE: Dance teacher, women's group speaker, abstinence educator in public and private schools.

BEST MOTIVATION FOR GETTING OUT OF BED: I am alive! I am thrilled that God has opened my eyes and I look forward to what He has for me each day. Plus, my dog, Bailey, wants to go for a run.

WHEN FRUSTRATED: I ask God to help me to remember that life's disappointments are His appointments, and He is in control. I spend time daily each morning praying, reading the Word and putting on my suit of armor to begin the day with God.

A MOVIE I WOULD WATCH OVER AND OVER: I love the movie "August Rush." The music and storyline are moving. I can watch the ending again and again. My favorite line is, "the music is all around us; why doesn't everybody hear it? Not everybody is listening."

THE WORLD WOULD BE A BETTER PLACE IF: Each person would value life, value the Giver of life, trust Christ as their Lord and Savior and treat others as they would want to be treated.

RECOMMENDATION: Frank Valenti, Senior Youth Leader, Hereford United Methodist Church

"We were looking for an inspirational speaker to start off our 'Speaker Series' at our new Family Life Center. We had heard that Mrs. Smith was a gifted speaker and her ministry topic contained all the latest and detailed subject matter that we wanted to present to our youth group. After contacting Mrs. Smith, we set a date for the event. Throughout the entire process of coordinating start times, audio visual, hands-on presentations, etc., she was extremely helpful and intuitive into what we were trying to teach our young people. Her presentation and demonstrations with the audience participation helped to make the subject matter flow smoothly and kept the energy levels high enough to keep our teens focused and attentive for over three hours!
We cannot express how much we appreciate the time and patience that she gave to our young people while talking about a subject that every teen should know. We sincerely recommend that every school, church, child agency, should contact Mrs. Smith to schedule an evening of fun and fellowship to help our teens discover what the truth is all about!"

19
Dance of a Wounded Warrior

"I'LL WATCH YOU DANCE"
Holly Starr

Hold down your hands and close your eyes
Trust Me this time; I've got something in mind
Don't try to guess or you'll miss it altogether
The timing's more important to Me anyways
And I'll watch you dance
When you see the plans I've made for us
When you take My hand
(I love you)

I like that smile I see on your face
It shows Me where you heart is and you've given Me a place
And when life starts changing, please don't run away
Hide in My arms and you will be saved

And I'll watch you dance
When you see the plans I've made for us
When you take My hand
(I love you)

Never in a million years would I have believed that our daughter, Nicole, and our son-in-law, Mike, would experience the excitement of two pregnancies and then harnessed to having to endure the heavy, burdensome walk through the valley of death with the loss of their longed-for babies.

Nicole & Mike had been trying to get pregnant for two and a half years. Achieving a successful conception was uncertain since she was diagnosed with polycystic ovarian syndrome. So, we were faithfully praying that Nicole would be able to conceive.

We ushered in 2013 by meeting with Nicole and Mike for coffee at a local bookstore upon their request. We settled into the coffee area of the bookstore waiting for them to arrive and I just knew they were going to be telling us that she was pregnant. I could barely contain my joy. Gary didn't want to get his hopes up too high. But Gary wandered through the store a bit and found a book of baby names and hid it at our table. As we sat waiting, we saw them float by the storefront window, giddy and rushing into the Big Lots store which was attached to the Books-A-Million where we were waiting. I knew they were buying something that either had 'Grandparents' or 'Grandmom' inscribed on it.

As they joined us, their faces were radiantly luminous and their joy was almost tactile. Nicole slid the thrown-together gift bag across the table and I ripped into it promptly revealing a picture frame that largely declared - Grandparents! I shouted, *"You're PREGNANT!"* The normally quiet coffee area filled with people relaxing, visiting and reading had their quietude temporarily interrupted. But most raised their eyes and smiled as they were witnesses to an obviously surprising and joyous moment for some strangers sharing public space together that evening.

Nicole immediately cautioned, *"You can't tell anyone."* Oops! How in the world was I going to contain myself? I had been preparing for this day for a long, long time. I was so ready to be 'Grandma.' The tap shoes, leotards, pink tutus; well, I was wishing for a little girl to whom I could teach tap.

We each returned home that evening and I was so high on joy that I could not sleep. I lie there dreaming of what would be; counting the months, preparing in my mind the baby shower and imagining the first time my eyes would behold my first grandchild at the nursery of the hospital. Upon seeing the sonogram of Nicole's first baby, I nicknamed it *Baby Bean*, because it looked like a little bean.

A few weeks later Nicole went for her third-month checkup. Afterwards, she called to tell me that they couldn't detect a heartbeat for the baby. She encouraged me not to worry because we had to remember that she had a tilted womb, so the doctor wanted to follow up with a sonogram. This was delivered to me by a voice message, which I picked up between my tap classes on a Thursday night. My heart and emotions immediately plummeted. I knew. I just knew. She was going to miscarry. I had been through this before. I ran out of the room and grabbed a parent and asked them to take over the class for me.

I broke down as if I had been punched in the gut and I could barely breathe. It was so hard to catch my breath. Later that night, my fears and intuition were confirmed. Nicole had to make the choice whether to miscarry naturally or schedule a D & E. The next day my baby girl went in for a D & E. She emerged with nothing to hold and lots of pain and agonizing emotions that followed. Another difficult part was that even though she had not yet felt life moving inside of her, she *embraced the understanding* of her baby's life forming inside. Now, everything was stripped away. Many months of physical and emotional healing ensued for Nicole and Mike; for all of us. This was a dance unlike any other - now my child was grieving and I couldn't do anything but pray.

One night, several months later, while playing a game of "Phase 10," Nicole blurted out, "I'm pregnant!" to which Gary and I both looked up and said, "Are you serious or just kidding?" She assured her seriousness... I was joyful, but apprehensive. After what had happened, which wasn't all that long before, none of us wanted to get our hopes up. We maintained a guarded joy.

Month one's checkup went well. All the counts looked good. Month two's sonogram went well and we could hear the heartbeat! Yay! Being present at month three's sonogram, I was able to watch the baby move and, with difficulty containing excitement, I gratefully gazed upon the baby's beating heart! Yay, again! The fourth month's sonogram should enable us to know the sex of the baby. However, Nicole and Mike did not want to know the sex of the baby and the really funny thing was that no matter which way Nicole positioned herself the technician was unable to get a view identifying the baby's sex. It was almost as if the baby was saying - *Well, since you don't want to know, I'll make it easy for you. I'm not going to show you.*

Things were going well for Nicole and every time I saw her, I would rub her belly and talk into her belly button and say, "Hi, Baby Bubble; Grandma is here." I had prayed that God would put a bubble of protection around this baby. Nicole would be gracious to me even though I don't think she liked me calling the baby, *Baby Bubble*. I just knew it was a girl.

During Nicole's first pregnancy, when *Baby Bean* miscarried, I finally had to accept that God knew something that we did not. During this new pregnancy, I was praying that this baby would be "to have and to hold."

Several weeks after month four, our family was looking forward to our annual pilgrimage to the Outer Banks of North Carolina, a privilege lovingly given to us by our dear friends, Frank and Flo. Mike and Nicole had just finished the baby's room and posted pictures on Facebook before we left for our trip. A couple of baby showers were planned and coming together smoothly. Gary and I had also fixed up a room in our home for the baby's visits: swing, pack and play, stroller and blankets. Everything was ready to go!

The Lord knew what would happen on Wednesday, September 18th, while we were on vacation at the Outer Banks; our favorite spot on Earth to spend our time together as a family. When Nicole first arrived at the beach, I bent down and said, "This is your first trip to the beach, Baby Bubble," and she loved the beach so much that she made her entrance into the world in the Outer Banks. She will always be our beach baby! I am still trying to wrap my mind around the fact that God knew this all along.

After we were all settled at the beach house, we were relaxing in the pool talking about our forthcoming grandchild and so excited for the time of year the baby was due – January 29, 2014. This winter date made it a good time to stay inside and fully enjoy the baby before springtime arrived.

On Tuesday of our vacation, Mike, Nicole and I took a ride into Duck, North Carolina, to explore the shops. While still in the car, I asked Nicole if she was going to take birthing classes. She responded that she didn't think so. I said, "There are many things you want to know before you go into labor." She said, "Like what?" I replied, "Like, did you know that you have to push the afterbirth out after you have the baby? Did you know that when you go into labor the hospital will only give you ice chips?" We continued talking for a while, but there was no way of knowing that within 24 hours of our sharing together that Nicole would be experiencing the need for that information.

Later that evening while eating dinner, Nicole said she wasn't feeling well. She was having tightness and cramping. I told her to call her doctor back home and they told her to rest. We started playing a game of "Phase 10" again but stopped because she was so uncomfortable. We decided to pop in the movie "The Natural" starring Robert Redford to see if that might calm things down. More than halfway through the movie, I could tell that Nicole was struggling and in pain. I whispered to her, "Let's go into the bedroom next to the family gathering area and talk." She explained that the tightness was coming regularly. I was greatly concerned. I didn't want to look worried, but I was frantic inside. I said, "Let's time the contractions." They were every three minutes and lasting 30 seconds. I said, "Let's call the doctor. We are an hour away from the nearest hospital. You are either in false labor or we need to get you checked out." The panic and adrenaline kicked in.

All four of us loaded into the car and Gary took off like an Indy racecar driver coursing around the windy two-lane road towards Nags Head. The normally one-hour trip became a 45-minute trip of terror. I couldn't talk. I just kept praying. My heart was pounding. I could hear Nicole in pain. What do you do when you can't do anything but pray? You pray!!! This was a very difficult dance that I did not want to do!

After arriving at the hospital and following the completion of Nicole's examination, a nurse gave her a diagnosis that she was dehydrated and needed to get fluids into her. They also attributed the cramping to the dehydration. She rested for a while and they gave her the option to go back to the beach house to rest or she could stay the night. They were able to hear the heartbeat of the baby, so we felt like she was in the clear. She was discharged.

We all regained our composure, mellowed a bit and started laughing assuming we were out of the danger-zone. But Nicole remained quiet. She later told me that she was still in pain. About 15 minutes into the return trip, she nervously yelled, "My water broke." As she placed her hand inside her pants she screamed, "Oh, no! It is blood." That was it! I cried out to God, "Oh, Sweet Jesus – not again!" I stared out the door as Gary whipped the car around and back onto the racetrack we went.

It was now about midnight, Wednesday, September 18, 2013. They readmitted Nicole into the hospital and moved her to the OB section. As we waited through the longest two hours of our lives, we could hear her screams echoing down the hallways. We weren't able to get any answers because the on-call doctor was not on the hospital premises but was now enroute.

Mike finally came out to update us and informed us, "Nicole is going to have the baby. The baby will not live (at 21 weeks, its lungs aren't developed enough) and Nicole might need a blood transfusion if she is bleeding internally." I cried out to the Lord and said, "In the name of Jesus, she will not need a blood transfusion!" Also, Mike needed to make the decision as to whether they wanted to see the baby, have the baby taken away or have the baby stay with them until she died, which could take anywhere from a few minutes to a couple of hours.

I couldn't process all of this! My head was spinning. I wanted to whisk Nicole off to another hospital two hours away by Medivac helicopter, but the baby was already in the birth canal. We could still hear Nicole screaming in the distance. I kept crying out to God, "Why? Why? Why?!" By now, it was 3am. It is just Gary and me at this time sitting and praying in the waiting room of an unfamiliar hospital far from home.

Gary got up and strolled around ending up at a nurse's station where a nurse was reading a Christian book by Stormie Omartian. Gary asked her to please pray for our daughter and Mike. It was truly comforting to know that God had people lined up to pray. I was, honestly, at a loss for words. I could have called to have a million people pray, but I was frozen in time. I felt paralyzed; enveloped in one of the darkest times of my life. Our dreams were tragically dashed. Our daughter would not be a mom. We would not be grandparents. Still . . . I asked God, *"Why?!"*

Mike returned to us in the waiting room looking very solemn. He said, "Nicole had the baby." As I leaned forward on the edge of my chair I replied, "She did?" He said, "It was a girl." I slumped down over the chair as I cried out to God, "Not a girl!" as every ounce of energy drained from my being. I wanted to teach tap to my granddaughter. I knew deep inside it was a girl! I was one of the only ones who said it was a girl! He said Nicole did not need a blood transfusion. Praise God!

I sneaked back to Nicole's room to try to see Nicole and the baby. As I walked into the room, almost in slow motion, Nicole was sound asleep in bed, escaping the consciousness of the pain and Mike's hands held the baby wrapped in a receiving blanket. I made my way toward Mike and looked down at our first-born granddaughter. She was perfectly formed in every way, just a miniature size. As I leaned forward to talk to her, I said, "Grandma will tap with you, sweet baby, in Heaven one day." My heart skipped as she slightly turned her head toward my voice. I gasped and broke down and cried. "Oh, my God, this is too much to take in! She recognized my voice." All those times I talked to her in the womb; it was as if she was responding to me.

As Mike handed my granddaughter to me, Nicole began to wake up. She said, "Mom, she has my nose, my fingers and toes. She has Mike's ears and mouth." I couldn't believe my eyes as I peered down closer scanning her ultra-petite features. She really did have Nicole's nose; it was just miniature. She always said that she hoped her babies wouldn't have her pug nose, as she would call it. But our little granddaughter did have Nicole's nose. It was beautiful!

Nicole said, "Mom, we named her Canon." I said to Mike, "Please go get Gary. I think he will be able to handle seeing her. And he'll regret it if he doesn't." Gary wasn't sure what he would see and thought he might not want that image in his mind. As Mike went to get Gary, I covered Canon in the bassinet with blankets and watched her try to breathe. I remember two weeks before she was born, when Nicole told me the names they had picked out for a boy and a girl; Canon was mentioned. I tried not to say too much, but my thought was - *Oh?* My first impression was that this little girl would always be asked why did your parents name you Canon? But, staring at her in her hospital bassinet and looking at her little bruised head and perfectly shaped body, I called out her name . . . *"Canon."* She was beautiful. It fit her well. I loved her and loved her name. She did come into the world like a cannon.

No one else was in the room with Nicole but the nurse scurrying around to relocate Nicole to another room. The pain had beckoned Nicole back to sleep again. I began singing to Canon, "Jesus loves me this I know, for the Bible tells me so. Little ones to Him belong. They are weak, but He is strong." Never . . . did those words in that song mean so much than at that moment! I also sang to her the song my Grandmother Kyte used to sing to me all the time: "You are my sunshine, my only sunshine. You make me happy when skies are gray. You'll never know, dear, how much I love you. So, please don't take my sunshine away."

I couldn't bear knowing she was still alive, so I told Canon, "It is okay, sweet baby, to go into the arms of Jesus!" At first, it seemed like 30 minutes of cruelty that she was born alive just to have us all wait for her to take her last breath. I couldn't believe that the God who works all things together for my good and the good of our family would allow us to suffer this almost unbearable hardship. As time has now passed, I see it as moments of blessing with our little, precious granddaughter; brief, but blessed. I believe it was God's gift to us – the privilege to actually see and touch her. It has been a bitter-sweet trial, but a divine privilege to hold my precious granddaughter and to sing to her during the first *and* last 30 minutes of her life.

I embrace the fact that we will spend eternity together someday, which brings some comfort. Canon is with Paisley who preceded her by miscarriage. Our little dancers are safe in the arms of Jesus. I will treasure Canon deep within my heart and long to see her and Paisley welcome me on the day I enter into heaven. I will know them.

As we were all trying to regain "strength for today and bright hope for tomorrow"(from the hymn "Great Is Thy Faithfulness") we were pressing forward and trusting God for an outcome that would bring Him glory.

Many months later, after the constant pain and tears of the loss of Canon, I grappled with God and said, "I need a name for the next pregnancy." Even though Nicole was not pregnant, nor ready to be again, I needed something to hope for. As I sat in my blue leather chair (where I have my quiet time) in the room I have designated the grandchild room, I begged God to give me my next grandchild's nickname. A thought popped into my head. "*RAISIN.*" What? Was that God or me? Raisin. I thought . . . like a tiny raisin? Then I felt as if a reply came. "No. This is the one she will be raisin (raising)! I couldn't wait to tell Gary! But I was reluctant to tell Nicole because everything was still so fresh. So, it is! I had begun praying for our third grandchild, *"Baby Raisin."* And we were waiting for the time for him/her to be placed into Nicole's womb or grafted into her family. Many years later, Nicole conceived during Covid. Baby Hope was who we prayed for, but in God's Sovereign plan she was to be with Him.

Sometimes the fairytale dream of being fruitful may be an emotional roller coaster that takes years. It may be that you encounter an unexpected pregnancy when you think that the timing could not have been worse. But God is still in control and does "work all things together for our good." My friend, Lisa, always quotes a declaration to me when I am struggling with a difficult trial: "Remember. God is NOT ALMOST SOVEREIGN."

One thing I do know is that God is continually showing me that when there is nothing I can do... pray. I cannot make things happen for Nicole and Mike even though I want so much to help it happen for them. IT HAS TO BE TOTALLY GOD!

"Hope dances in the puddles 'til the sun comes out again."
(Author Unknown)

20
Dance with a Bully

Woundedness comes in all shapes and sizes and happens at any age and is just as distressing regardless of age. When I was in sixth grade, for some reason unknown to me, I was labeled as the *teacher's pet*. I'm not sure if it was because I was a high achiever or because I liked to stay after school to help the teacher. There was a boy in my class named Johnny. Whenever the teacher left the room, Johnny would walk up to my desk and begin to pound my desk with his fist with the same rhythm: pump-pump-pa-dump-pump, then turn and smack me across the face. The class would erupt into laughter. I just took it – not just for one day, but for many!

Finally, after a couple of weeks, I got the nerve to confront him. When the teacher left the room, Johnny started his approach toward me and I could feel my heart race faster and faster. Sweat began to run down my neck. As Johnny began his pump-pump-pa-dump-pump beat on my desk and as he began to raise his hand, I caught it and stopped him in action. I told him, "Meet me after school. We are going to settle this!" Johnny wimped out and never did meet me, but he also never came by my desk again!

That same year a small gang of kids that hated me for being the teacher's pet followed me home from school chanting the whole time. Boy! Was I ever scared! My Mother had drilled into my head that because of the epilepsy I needed to be so careful not to get into a fight. I didn't have a fighting bone in my body. The stronger kids pick on those perceived as weaker ones. My husband says it is like the animal kingdom's pecking order. So, I would say that God protected me when they threw not only accusations, but items such as rocks and whatever else they thought would scare me. And it did.

The funny thing is, that if I attended a school reunion, I would probably remember each person as the bully they were, even if they had become Christians sometime during the following years. Those kinds of malicious incidents create deep-rooted, dreadful memories which are difficult to shake. But as we give over our stash of hurtful memories and mistreatments to the Lord, He is able to take away the sting in those memories enabling us to have those recollections, now, free of the pain.

During my darkest and dry seasons of loneliness as an empty-nester, the loss of the grandbabies and the struggles in life, I turned to the Scriptures where God has provided to us words of solace and encouragement when we need them. Here are some edifying passages that lifted me up. Perhaps they will encourage you, too!

> "The Lord says, 'I will give you back what you lost to the swarming locusts,
> the hopping locusts, the stripping locusts, and the cutting locusts . . .'"
> (Joel 2:25)

"A servant of the Lord must not quarrel but must be kind to everyone, be able to teach, and be patient with difficult people. Gently instruct those who oppose the truth. Perhaps God will change those people's hearts, and they will learn the truth. Then they will come to their senses and escape from the devil's trap. For they have been held captive by him to do whatever he wants."
(II Timothy 2:24-26)

"Even though the fig trees have no blossoms, and there are no grapes on the vines; even though the olive crop fails, and the fields lie empty and barren; even though the flocks die in the fields, and the cattle barns are empty, yet I will rejoice in the Lord! I will be joyful in the God of my salvation! The Sovereign Lord is my strength! He makes me as surefooted as a deer, able to tread upon the heights." (Habakkuk 3:17-19)

Whatever is going on in your life right now, BE ENCOURAGED IN THE LORD! God is not finished with your dance and continues to choreograph each step for His glory.

MOVING ON

After a crisis, it is human to need a break; time off. It's a recovery time the length of which is different for each person. Months, months and more months passed with the unfinished manuscript of my book cast aside by hands, mind and emotions too battered to pen even one word. I literally needed to stop everything after Canon's passing to Heaven. At the same time, I was dealing with some ongoing family struggles. It was just too much. I needed time to deal with all the pain, depression, anger, grief, disappointment, despair, frustration, disbelief, self-pity and jealousy. What a barrage of emotions! Some days I never wanted my feet to hit the floor in the mornings. All I did was eat and sleep. I don't recall ever having dealt with this depth of heartache in my life.

After having expended all possible tears and having entered a dry-eye time where I could finally sit and reflect on the pain without crying, God began to draw me back to write. Gary was getting ready for work one day and said in a careful, but stern admonition, *"It's time to get back to your book! People need to hear your story."* I knew Gary was right-on, because God had spoken to my soul the prior day as I was reading II Samuel 12, the story of David's baby son who died. The Lord spoke to my heart saying, *"The time of grieving is over, Cheryl. It is time to get up, wash your face and worship ME!"*

That chapter spoke directly to my heart. Please take the time to read it for yourself.

"The Lord sent Nathan to David. When he came to David, he said, 'There were two men in a city. One was rich, but the other was poor. The rich man had many sheep and cattle. But the poor man had nothing except one little female lamb he had bought. The poor man fed the lamb and it grew up with him and his children. It shared his food and drank from his cup and slept in his arms. The lamb was like a daughter to him. Then a traveler stopped to visit the rich man. The rich man wanted to feed the traveler, but he didn't want to take one of his own sheep or cattle. Instead, he took the lamb from the poor man and cooked it for his visitor.'

David became very angry at this rich man. He said to Nathan, 'As surely as the Lord lives, the man who did this should die! He must pay for the lamb four times for doing such a thing. He had no mercy!'

Then Nathan said to David, 'You are the man! This is what the LORD, the God of Israel says: 'I appointed you king of Israel and saved you from Saul. I gave you his kingdom and his wives. And I made you king of Israel and Judah. And if that had not been enough, I would have given you even more. So why did you ignore the LORD'S command? Why did you do what he says is wrong? You killed Uriah the Hittite with the sword of the Ammonites and took his wife to be your wife! Now there will always be people in your family who will die by a sword, because you did not respect Me; you took the wife of Uriah the Hittite for yourself!'

This is what the LORD says: 'I am bringing trouble to you from your own family. While you watch, I will take your wives from you and give them to someone who is very close to you. He will have sexual relations with your wives and everyone will know it. You had sexual relations with Bathsheba in secret, but I will do this so all the people of Israel can see it.'

Then David said to Nathan, 'I have sinned against the LORD.'

Nathan answered, 'The LORD has taken away your sin. You will not die. But what you did caused the LORD'S enemies to lose all respect for Him. For this reason, the son who was born to you will die.' Then Nathan went home.

And the LORD caused the son of David and Bathsheba, Uriah's widow, to be very sick. David prayed to God for the baby. David fasted and went into his house and stayed there, lying on the ground all night. The elders of David's family came to him and tried to pull him up from the ground, but he refused to get up or to eat food with them.

On the seventh day the baby died. David's servants were afraid to tell him that the baby was dead. They said, 'Look, we tried to talk to David while the baby was alive, but he refused to listen to us. If we tell him the baby is dead, he may do something awful.'

When David saw his servants whispering, he knew that the baby was dead. So, he asked them, 'Is the baby dead' They answered, 'Yes, he is dead.'

Then David got up from the floor, washed himself, put lotions on, and changed his clothes. Then he went into the LORD'S house to worship. After that, he went home and asked for something to eat. His servants gave him some food and he ate.'

David's servants said to him, 'Why are you doing this? When the baby was still alive, you fasted and you cried. Now that the baby is dead, you get up and eat food.'

David said, 'While the baby was still alive, I fasted and I cried. I thought, who knows? Maybe the LORD will feel sorry for me and let the baby live. But now that the baby is dead, why should I fast? I can't bring him back to life. Someday I will go to him, but he cannot come back to me.'

Then David comforted Bathsheba his wife. He slept with her and had sexual relations with her. She became pregnant again and had another son, whom David named Solomon. The LORD loved Solomon. The LORD sent word through Nathan the prophet to name the baby Jedidiah, because the LORD loved the child."

Through all of this trauma, I wanted so desperately to get back to *normal,* or at least close to it, and as I searched my heart, I heard the Lord gently counseling me that my children and grandchildren had become IDOLS (anything I put before my God) in my life. I would have never imagined that I was able to worship my children or grandchildren. But it was true. My mind was consumed with my children and my excessive desire to be a grandparent. They had all taken the place of my devotion to God.

I had robbed God of way too much time by staying consumed with things I could not change. I had become my own 'pillar of salt' (Genesis 19:26). Lot's wife, a disobedient woman turned into a pillar of salt for looking back to see the destruction of Sodom and Gomorrah. It was time to STOP looking back! Because of this obsession, I even came to the place where I just didn't want to go on. I would never take my own life, but I was frequently crying out to God to take it for me; to take me Home.

I knew God was patient with me and my temper tantrums. He didn't let it go that I was neglecting to finish my book, but He also didn't chastise me. He just continued to unconditionally love me in this very difficult dance. Wow! What a kind and understanding God we serve! I wanted to be obedient to His call in my life to complete this book. So, I moved on; I plowed ahead to finish what God had asked me to do.

This verse dumbfounds me: *"Don't you see how wonderfully kind, tolerant, and patient God is with you? Does this mean nothing to you? Can't you see that His kindness is intended to turn you from your sin?"* (Romans 2:4) I did not realize that fighting God and struggling in this part of my dance was sin! Why would I wrestle with God? Who lost the battle? Me! I lost time. I allowed myself to let the enemy steal, kill and destroy my peace, joy, courage and mission. (John 10:10)

Several years later, God answered Nicole & Mike's heart to have a child. They walked through the process of adopting a little girl, Adeline Hazel. After six days, the mother decided to take her back. In Pennsylvania, you have a month to change your mind after you give the baby up at birth. Yet another deep wound and test like never before! How could one person go through so much? My heart was breaking for my daughter and son-in-law and I could not fix it or make it happen. But God later blessed them with a divine intervention from a private adoption. Our Isaiah came to us and is now grafted into the family. What a beautiful picture of how God grafted us into His family! We have since been blessed to have three beautiful grandchildren: Ocean, Azalea and Nova from Matt & Skye. God has answered my prayers and being a grandmother is one of the most rewarding dances ever. He takes our wounds and heals them in His Time and in His Way!

When teaching my dancers life lessons, I am brutally honest in sharing my experiences with them. Peer pressure and the *bullies* of life will always be around at every phase and age. I encourage them to stand strong in who they are in Christ; don't be swayed and stay the course. Never let the Bully Win!

21
Keep Dancing
No Matter What

When life threw me curve balls and took my soul down a long dark night (written about by Oswald Chambers), Amanda Cook's song "Heroes" ministered to my heart as I was dealing with great disappointments in my life, family and ministry. She sings, "You taught me to dance upon disappointment." I never like disappointment... my expectations dashed. Who does? Sometimes, it is SOOO dark and you wonder if there is any light at the end of the proverbial tunnel? Corrie Ten Boom said, "When a train goes through a tunnel and it gets dark, you don't throw away the ticket and jump off, you sit still and trust the engineer." Sometimes I wanted to jump off my train! I do not always like the ride I am on but I have to trust my engineer. He knows where I need to go. By the way - this ticket is FREE!

A woman I greatly respect and followed in my early Christian walk is Elizabeth Elliot. One of my favorite quotes from her is "Don't dig up in doubt what you planted in faith." Praying and believing is harder than ever when our faith is challenged through life's unexpected twists and turns. R.A. Torrey said, "The chief purpose of prayer is that God may be glorified in the answer."

My sister-in-law, Cindy, is an artist. She cross-stitches Christmas stockings and wall hangings. I have always admired her patience as she intricately works the tiny threads together. She has shown me the process of all the threads entangled on the back of each tapestry. It looks like a giant mess to me! But when the fabric is turned over to the other side and she shows what the finished product looks like, I am breathtakingly amazed! Trusting God with the loose threads of our brokenness as He weaves His tapestry is not an easy process on us, but our Master Artist knows exactly what He is working to accomplish with our cooperation, and the end product will be a unique Masterpiece!

In life, when I expected something to go a certain way and it didn't, I hit rock bottom. My friend, Flo, would tell me to *have no expectations, then* I would not be disappointed. That almost seemed impossible. God began to train me not to expect anything from anyone *BUT HIM* and His Promises! Kay Arthur writes about "our disappointments as His appointments." This is oftentimes a hard pill to swallow. Are you ever frustrated? My expectations of people and my calendar of events that did not happen became my frustrations. It seemed I frequently set myself up for a fall.

I have danced through depression, not understanding God's sovereignty in my life as well as in the life of my family. I looked around at others and envied or coveted the things they had that I did not. Things welled up in my heart I never knew I could feel. How was I going to process those feelings? My wandering in the desert was like struggling to break out of a cocoon. I wanted to fly, but I couldn't. My life verse remains:

> *"But those who wait on the Lord shall renew their strength. They shall mount up with wings like eagles, they shall run and not be weary, they shall walk and not faint." (Isaiah 40:31).*

How I felt like fainting many days! But God renewed my mind through His Word as I read it and it strengthened me to *"WALK,"* then *"Run and Not be Weary!"* God reminded me of a writing by V. Raymond Edman: "Never doubt in the dark what God told you in the light."

This Christian walk is not a sprint, but a marathon. I have never been a runner, but my son, Matt, is. He competes in triathlons. It amazes me to see him along with many others swim, bike and run with utter ease. They set their minds towards the goal and the finish line. The writer of the book of Hebrews, gives us very sound spiritual understanding.

> *"Therefore, since we are surrounded by such a great cloud of witnesses, let us throw off everything that hinders and the sin that so easily entangles. And let us run with perseverance the race marked out for us." (Hebrews 12:1)*

It is so difficult to run much less walk, or even get out of bed, when you face the death of a loved one, loss of a job, health issues, and everyday relationship challenges. I believe, with all my heart, if the enemy is able to obstruct your dance, he can quickly steal your joy! In Patsy Clairmont's book, "Twirl - A Fresh Spin at Life," she pens her final page with a poem.

"GROWING UP"
Stephanie Eddleman

> *Growing up I was not allowed to dance.*
> *I was given a long list of reasons why,*
> *None of which belong in a poem.*
> *But I've seen babies dance and birds pirouette and horses prance*
> *I've seen sailboats waltz with the ocean*
> *Why, even runaway plastic bags leap and twirl in the wind!*
> *When the spirit dances, will the body follow?*

Some have never danced; some were not permitted to dance due to religious upbringing and some have been hindered in the dance! Watching a child dance is breathtaking, as they have no fear, no inhibitions, no restrictions and dance *freely*! It comes naturally. I love to worship the Lord through singing and dance. Jared Anderson in his song "Inside" sings, *"And give our children freedom to dance again, they will dance again."*

Since 2004, I have had the privilege of teaching ballet and tap in the county in which we live - York, Pennsylvania. I love the quote by Tim Challies, *"No matter what my work is, it matters, because my work is a stage to bring glory to my God."* How many people actually love their work? When you don't see it as just a job, then you will love that dance. I LOVE My work!

Recently I received the gift of a candle from a young girl, Gracelyn. On it was inscribed *"Behind every dancer who believes in themselves is a teacher who believed in them first!"* Miss Jean Kettell, my childhood dance instructor, believed in me and gave me wings to soar in dance and imparted a wealth of knowledge that has enabled me to teach every hungry student who enters our studio – teaching the joy of dancing to those whose hearts long to know the wonderment it offers. Each one will have the same possibilities that I had and decide how dance will fit into their lives. What is beyond my comprehension is that Miss Jean is still teaching dance in her eighties! I can only hope I will be able to do the same. She is my inspiration. Miss Jean's life spurs me on, keeping the flame of dancing and teaching alive within me.

I can remember all of my dance shoes I've ever worn over my lifetime - ballet, jazz, Hermes sandals, pointe, character, and my favorite of all - tap shoes! My husband often says, "Don't wear the wrong shoes to the dance!" as an illustration when teaching. Wearing the wrong shoes in life can make life harder. I know I have used stiletto heels to look fashionable for weddings and paid the price with blisters and foot pain. Feet are interesting - not the prettiest part of our bodies. But Jesus says, *"How beautiful are the feet of messengers who bring good news*!" (Romans 10:15) I want feet like that!

Author and motivational speaker, Vivian Greene, wrote, *"Life isn't about waiting for the storm to pass; it's about learning to dance in the rain."* In every season of life, no matter which shoes you wear, whether new, worn-out or stretched, *it's time to dance again.* It's not always easy to get our shoes on. You know what I mean? I find that the older I get, bending over to get my shoes on gets a little more challenging (ha ha). The greatest challenges in life can come through the people we have loved the most. No matter what situation springs up to discourage us, depress us or the actions of people who knowingly or unknowingly try to deflate us, loving God more will help us to stay in the dance. So, get up. Get your dancing shoes on and start afresh. You never know what dances may still lie ahead.

In the past few years, traversing through the death of both parents, my faithful friend, Flo, and my walking partner, Bailey, life has changed so much. When our son, Josh, decided to fulfill his dreams to live in California, I was challenged once again with change, which I do not easily dance well with. When the steps of the dance come in ways we don't necessarily have control over and when we deal with the loss of family, whether by a vocational move, heartache in relationship or Heaven, we need to know how to *keep dancing.*

I never thought I would get to experience the West Coast, but when our son, Josh, took off across the country in his tiny Toyota Matrix on March 28, 2021, I wasn't sure if he would be back to the East Coast any time soon. His motto: "Go Big or Go Home." Since the date he moved to the Pacific side of our great nation, we had only seen Josh for 30 minutes when we traveled to Philadelphia to see him at a Red Bull event that he was filming for his pro-skater friend, Chris Chann. That hug didn't last long enough, so we decided to catch Southwest Airlines to Los Angeles, California, on March 28, 2023 - the exact day he drove away two years earlier. We so anticipated seeing our son, meeting his girlfriend, Morgan, and exploring as many places as possible in four days!

I've got to share with you some special memories I will never forget like walking with Josh to get coffee, shopping, talking and catching up. Josh made dinner for us with his fabulous Yo's Cheesesteaks Philly-style. He treated his dad and me for our 45th Anniversary to a high-end restaurant, Olivetta, in West Hollywood. He was so excited to purchase a cute floral romper for me to wear for this special night out. Morgan accessorized it with a fun white jean jacket from her closet to complete the outfit. Josh drove me by the Michael Jackson Thriller home. As we advanced up the hill in the dark of night, it was a bit eerie. It still looked exactly the same when the MTV video came out on December 2, 1983. I jumped out of the car, as Morgan turned the volume up to the Thriller song. Josh took a 30-second clip of me in front of the house slipping back in time with some of the dance moves from the original dance. I just had to! No one was out and about in the area but, even if they were, I still would have done it. Give me any chance to dance and I will.

Our first trip to California was fast and furious. In just four days, we captured the majestic snow-capped mountains surrounding the valley, scaled the mansions in Beverly Hills, toured the quaint town of Pasadena, flashy Hollywood, peaceful Glendale with The Americana at Brand elite shopping, Deus Ex Machina of Venice Beach where Josh landed his first job, and Los Angeles. We had super fun times singing Ventura Highway on Ventura Highway, tailgated Target Tacos, Foxy's Restaurant in Glendale with a toaster on the table, climbed various rocks at Malibu Beach, cruised the Coastal highway, Sunset Strip, Burbank Studios where we remember watching "The Price is Right" and "The Johnny Carson Show" on TV, adored the palm trees and bright colored exotic succulents, savored the best donuts ever at Donut Friend in Highland Park, enjoyed Griffith Observatory and adored the city lights at night. As we were ubered by Josh and Morgan all over town, all of these places we had seen in pictures, on Facetime, in movies and television came to life. But even if we had never seen all these wonderful places, just seeing Josh in his element was all we needed!

God is so good to allow us the opportunity to check off more boxes in our desires and dreams! He wants so much more for us in our dance than we dare to think, dream or imagine. (Ephesians 6:20)

Flying back home, as I peered through the miniature, glazed window and looked down at the sphere below me, I was reminded of just how vast God is. How does He know every single human being, the hairs on their head, where they are at every moment, their needs, their thoughts and desires, their future, their date of expiration, their health, their education or vocation, their spouse, children, private sin, history, the sins not yet committed, their tragedies, events yet to come? Wow! All of those thoughts still don't begin to even scratch the surface. I can't comprehend God!!! It's way too much to take in. His thoughts are not my thoughts.

> *"My thoughts are nothing like your thoughts, says the Lord. And My ways are far beyond anything you could imagine. For just as the heavens are higher than the earth, so My ways are higher than your ways and My thoughts higher than your thoughts." (Isaiah 55:8-9)*

My God is an Awesome God! I'm taking a memory sideroad here. My first Christian concert was attending a Rich Mullins night of worship in 1986. Rich was a contemporary Christian-music singer and songwriter best known for his worship-leading. I was a little perplexed when he walked out onto the platform of the church a few feet in front of us wearing a t-shirt, jeans and no shoes! That was a first for me. Oh my. My judgment of him was so wrong. He was so in-tune with God, and led us all to melt together as 'one' in worship that night. He opened the concert with the song "Awesome God," and I was ushered into the presence of God. Eleven years later, Rich entered the Kingdom of Heaven by way of a car accident. I wonder if God just wanted him singing that song by His side?

Back to adventures in California. Stopping in Malibu and seeing the Hollywood sign in person for the first time, I had to jump out of the car and get a snap shot of a popular dance pose. Morgan taking me to Chado Tea Room in Pasadena, California, for a traditional English Tea was a highlight, since she lived in London for the first few years of her life and wanted to share that experience with me.

So many times, we experience our 'first' dance in life through a prom, graduation, marriage, children, a place and the list goes on. Dancing through those times, realizing they are a part of the blessing and part of our story to pass down as a legacy, makes it all the more exhilarating.

Life is captivating as it waltzes by in 'light years.' The twists, turns, people that come and depart, the hopes and dreams, the disappointments, the unexpected blessings, roller coaster relationships, and heartaches. BUT, God. (My husband always says there are a lot of big BUT's in the bible - no pun intended.) Just when I think I have finally figured out life, God reminds me of His steadfast love, grace and mercy in my daily routine. The older I get (63 at the present), I realize that even though I sometimes reflect on the future and wonder how long I will be here, God has already ordained my time. I can't die one day before I am supposed to. That's comforting, if I choose to rest in Him and trust Him and not dance to the beat of my own drum of fear.

Fear will keep us from Dancing! Fear will paralyze us! Fear is not from God! Keep Dancing! You have the greatest Dance Partner in the game of life!

22
The Dance of Loss

March of 2020! Covid Pandemic Lockdown. It was predicted to last a few weeks, but became a two-year stretch for people all over the globe. Many people lost their lives, lost a loved one and some became very ill. We all have Covid stories as we have lived through a season in time like no other. We were required to wear masks, to ensure six-foot distancing, hospitals bursting at the seams, schools closed, stores closed, many funerals deferred, limited food and household supplies, children isolated and confused, many struggled with mental instability and many relationships were challenged. God was faithful to supply our needs through this severe time, as well and even some of the desires of our hearts.

When we could not go into the churches, due to them being shut down, God birthed a small group of believers. If it was not for our friends, Steve and Robin, who asked if we could do a Bible study with them, we may still be searching for a church. We call our group"The Gathering," and meet weekly to dig into God's Word and share life together. It is the closest model to Acts 2:42-47 we have experienced in the church. We are forever grateful for their bond of love and friendship. God met us where we were when we needed Him to get us back in the *dance* after a long desert experience since our church closed. He is bringing us healing, hope and a future through a ministry in a way we never could have dreamed. We praise Him for new beginnings.

During the first four weeks of the epidemic, my dad passed away. He did not die of the virus, but had cancer. I believe he gave up the will to fight when we were not allowed to go see him. The day after we found out that my dad was in the process of passing, I was able to get permission to see him for 10 minutes in the Nursing home to say goodbye. At that same time, my mom was diagnosed with Covid. I remember saying to God, "Not two in a week, Lord; please, don't take both." My mom weathered through Covid well, but my dad entered eternity that Tuesday on April 14th.

Dad should have had the celebration of a lifetime due to his network of friends and community influence (softball, card buddies, Newspaper co-workers and Senior Center companions). But instead, we were only allowed 10 family members to attend his funeral. How do you choose 10 people when you have children and grandchildren? It was so sad and unfair! He deserved so much better. I often say, "Dad, you picked the worst time to die!" Just sayin'. It was even harder to carry my dad's casket to the hearse. I would have never, in my entire life, dreamed his funeral would have been carried out this way.

Several years before my dad ended up in a nursing home, my mom developed dementia. We are not sure if it was a fall or a stroke which caused the onset. But when my dad went into the hospital for his cancer surgery, my mom did have a stroke.

Because she was not able to be without a caregiver 24/7, she was admitted to a permanent nursing home. My mom's dementia was extremely heavy on the heart! The sound mind is such a priceless thing. Dementia has robbed millions of precious people of countless hours and years of normal, cognitive life with family and friends.

A few weeks after my dad passed, our daughter, Nicole, lost her baby from an unexpected pregnancy. We had longed so much to welcome this baby into the family. Nicole named the baby, Hope. At the same time, our daughter-in-law, Skye, gave birth to a little girl, Nova, our shining star.

Several months later, I lost my spiritual mom, Florence Simansky, who mentored me from the day I became a Christian. I told her she could never die - I would need her forever. But she now enjoys her completed salvation. My life would not be the same without Flo's weekly and sometimes minute-by-minute friendship. Alex Haley said, "Every time an old person dies, it's as though a library has been burned." (From "Once Upon a Time: Discovering Our Forever After Story," by Debbie Macomber) When my friend passed, we all lost a gem in the library!

Death was just all around. One month later, my walking partner, Bailey, crossed over, what they call, The Rainbow Bridge. Everyone says their dog is the best, but Bailey was truly a "human dog." She was a pleaser, loved kids, always had a smile on her face and thoroughly loved life! When I was dripping with heartache and sorrow, she got me up when I couldn't get out of bed. The day we had to take her to the veterinarian, she walked with me on our routine landscape. It started to rain. "Bailey, let's run!" Bailey just stopped and looked at me. She could not run like she routinely did every other time. I KNEW something was wrong. I got back to the house and watched her as she was in pain. I did not know at that time that she had a tumor pressing on her stomach. I had to prepare myself, because I KNEW our trip would not be a return-trip home.

I did not know how I was going to face each day without having Bailey to get me up to walk. The day she passed, I texted my dancer friend Mariah. Mariah asked me, "What time do you walk in the morning?" I said 7:00 AM, I thought she was going to call me when I went on the walk. The next morning, I walked around the corner of my house to begin my walk, pulled out my phone expecting her call but when I looked up she was walking up my driveway to walk with me! I was in *shock!* I cried and gave her a hug. She blessed me beyond measure and I was able to walk without Bailey after that day. The measure of sacrificial love of a friend to go beyond, and journey with me through this loss meant more to me than I could express in words at the time.

How hard it is knowing the day will always come when we need to say goodbye. But when it happens, we struggle. How we struggle! God gives us pets for companionship. They show us an attribute of God that humans resist – unconditional love.

"A time to cry, and a time to laugh. A time to grieve and a time to dance."
(Ecclesiastes 3:4)

After reading "I Will Carry You - The Sacred Dance of Grief and Joy," by Angie Smith, I have a new appreciation for the dance of grief or the times when you cannot even utter a word. Angie is the wife of Todd Smith (lead singer of the Dove Award winning group Selah). Eighteen weeks into her pregnancy with her fourth daughter, Audrey Caroline, the doctors discovered conditions they determined would leave Audrey "incompatible with life." When Todd and Angie were faced with the unbearable decision whether to terminate the pregnancy or not, they decided to carry Audrey as long as she had life. Three pounds-two ounces, Audrey Caroline was born and lived for over two hours.

In Angie's book, she quotes Henri Nouwen from his book "Turn My Mourning into Dancing." She expresses the struggle to either resent what God allows in life or to be grateful. Henri Nouwen writes:

"Our choice, then, often revolves around not what has happened or will happen to us, but how we will relate to life's turns and circumstances. Put another way: Will I relate to my life resentfully or gratefully?"

Angie conveys, "But that's just it; I can either focus on what I have lost, or what I have gained, and so I choose the latter. Sometimes I have to choose it a couple times an hour." Henri Nouwen speaks to this need:

*"And so we wait patiently, if the situation requires it, watching for gifts to come where we are. Look at the wonderful, exuberant flowers painted by the famous Dutch artist Vincent van Gogh. What grief, what sadness, what melancholy he experienced in his difficult life! Yet what beauty, what ecstasy! Looking at his vibrant paintings of sunflowers, who can say where the mourning ends and the dance begins? Our glory is hidden in our pain, if we allow God to bring the gift Himself in our experience of it. If we turn to God, not rebelling against our hurt, we let God transform it with greater good. We let others join in and discover it with us. And herein lies the dance we will do for the rest of our lives. It is a dance that was begun before we were born, long before the music even began to play. What the Lord has given us can either be taken into ourselves as pain or given back to Him as a holy offering; one that glorifies His name and gives meaning to our loss.

If mourning and dancing are part of the same movement of grace, we can be grateful for every moment we have lived. We can claim our unique journey as God's way to mold our hearts to greater conformity to Christ. The cross, the primary symbol of our faith, invites us to see grace where there is pain; to see resurrection where there is death. The call to be grateful is a call to trust that every moment can be claimed as the way of the cross that leads to life."

In Angie's own grief she decided to take each moment and turn it toward the glory of God! She writes:

"In the months that have passed since we lost our Audrey, I have learned that grief is a dance. I do it rather clumsily much of the time, but as it turns out, I am in good company. Others who have lost children have shared the inability to separate the sorrow from the joy of life. I find that they are inextricably woven, never to be pulled fully from each other in this life. I am reminded of this delicate dance as I think upon the Savior whose blood mingled with our freedom. I am an injured dancer, and yet one who wants her life to bring glory to the one who allowed sorrow and joy to dance at all."

No matter what circumstances, trials, and pain we have gone through and will yet go through, God is able to give us the grace to persevere!

Even though you know it will eventually happen if we live long enough, we can anticipate losing a grandparent and parent. It is most unnatural to lose a

*I Will Carry You – The Sacred Dance of Grief and Joy; "Since She Left;" pp. 156-157

child/grandchild and is never expected. The dance of grief is the hardest to waltz to - its beat is foreign to us and it's hard to get into its step.

Two years and nine months after my dad passed and walked into Heaven, my mom followed. Around Christmas 2022, the hospice nurse gave us 3-6 months for Mom.

Each visit I had with her I accepted knowing the days were counting down till there would be no more. But I have seen many blessings of healing through this disease. We had never laughed so much, reminisced so much and just sat together without saying a word.

The dementia became a blessing for what mom would not know, while simultaneously being a curse for watching it eat away what memory she had. Mom accomplished so much in her lifetime. She earned her Bachelor of Science degree at Towson University in Political Science/Women's Studies. She also worked for the Baltimore County Department of Aging as a Community Outreach Specialist.

After Christmas, I was able to spend a day with her at the wonderful Carroll Lutheran Village in Westminster, Maryland. As I write this, I still can't believe it is all past tense so hard to process and is still surreal. You have a parent all your life. Then one day, the very real, but invisible, mother-daughter umbilical cord is cut once again. In the very beginning, when God created the Earth, He did not intend death to have any part in our lives. Oh! BUT EVE! How I intensely wish she had never taken a bite of that forbidden fruit! We will all suffer the loss of those around us, especially as the older years approach.

It was Sunday, January 29th, and my sister, Tanya, told me my mom was diagnosed with only having three to four days after contracting Covid. How devastating! My mom's time was going to be cut shorter than we had originally been told. I had planned to go on Tuesday and stay the day with my mom, but when I went to bed on Sunday, I had lain there and could not sleep. I questioned God. *Lord, what do I do? Do I wait?* I felt a tugging to text my sister who had been at the nursing home all day. I asked Tanya if I should go see mom now? Or wait? She told me mom was progressing quickly and she did not know how long she had. At that point, I knew I needed to go and not wait.

It was 11:00 p.m. and Gary asked me if I wanted him to drive me to see my mom. I was concerned about traveling an hour by myself on the dark wooded road where deer sometimes decide to dance out in front of a car. With Gary having to go to work at 5 a.m., and if Mom would pass while we were there, I did not want to have to leave. So, I hopped into the car and called my son, Josh, in California, and talked to him while I made the drive to see my mom. Because of the time-difference of three hours behind us (PST), he tracked my car route with 'Find my Friend' and helped me stay focused.

Upon arrival at the nursing home, I had to suit up in Covid protection with a body covering, gloves, N-95 mask and face shield. This brought back memories of how we had to go in to see my dad when we were allotted only 10 minutes with him three weeks after the March 2020 Covid lockdown. My mom had drastically lost weight in just a few days from the last day I had visited her. I arrived at midnight, January 30th. This day that had no significance before, would now be branded into my mind forever. My sister needed to leave around 2:00 a.m. after being all day by my mom's side.

God's grace danced all over my mom and me in the wee hours of the morning. I did not know while I was there alone if my mom could hear me, but I decided to speak to her and affirm all she had done for my family and me. I told her each person by name loved her, sang songs to her and played the best hymn-songs playlist on my phone to her and prayed she would go into Jesus' arms while I was with her. Each hour, I thought I would leave to go back home, because I did not know if I would be able to stay awake all night and then teach dance the next day. Each hour came and it was as if God said, don't leave. So, I planned to stay until my sister was able to return around 9:30 a.m. from work. In the early morning, I can only tell you that the GRACE of GOD was so very evident in the room my mom called home for the last three years. It dumbfounded me! I kept thinking I should be feeling so much sorrow, but God held me up and helped my mom in her final hours.

I left the nursing home to go home for sleep and a shower, and told my mom when I kissed her, "I will either see you here again or on the other-side." I came to grips with the probability that this was most likely the last time I would see my mom as I drove away. I was beyond exhausted with having been awake all night. I safely reached home - ate, showered and hit the bed for desperately needed sleep. I anticipated uninterrupted slumber for hours, but awoke suddenly out of my sleep and sensed I should check my phone. My sister had just called and I had missed it. I immediately called her back with anticipation laden with dread. I heard the words I will never forget, "Cheryl, Mom passed!" Everything changed! So hard to accept the realization of no more calls, laughs, visits, memories together and tap dancing for her and the residents of the home. A part of me hopes there are tap shoes in Heaven and now she is shuffling around with my dad and our grandchildren who preceded us!

When I walked into Duda-Ruck funeral home in Dundalk, my hometown in Baltimore, for my mom's viewing, her face looked like she had gone back in time. She looked at least 15 years younger. She was absolutely radiant. All her troubles, lack of memory, battle with self and confusion were over!

From my earliest memory of my mom, I learned so many meaningful things which were forged into the fabric of my being. To honor her, please indulge my desire to share some of her wonderful characteristics with you.

1. **DINNER TIME** - Meals are eaten together. Mom was a great cook, but a better baker! Her Cinnamon cake, Elvis Presley pound cake and pies were the hit of many family occasions.
2. **GROCERY SHOPPING** - She was the queen of coupons and getting the best deal from each store whether or not she had to use a tank of gas.
3. **ORGANIZATION** - Between my mom and dad these are some of the things I inherited: be on time (early is on time and on time is late); notes, notes and more notes to remember what you have to do; make a list from year to year to remember what you did for each holiday; Holidays - every holiday was celebrated with decorations, cards and gifts; Cleaning Day - my mom inherited this from my grandmother, Madeline. I was passed down to me and now my daughter, Nicole - once a week and spring/fall deep cleaning
4. **DECORATING** - Mom had a knack for making each room a designer room before there were shows like 'Fixer Upper,' Love it or List it,' 'Design on a Dime,' etc. My fairytale dream of purple walls, white wooden canopy bed and beautiful accents.
5. **GARDENING** - Mom loved floriculture. I never got the 'green thumb' from her, even though I appreciate all she taught me through her picturesque flower displays that she designed in her gardens.
6. HOME - Our home was the place for family parties, celebrations, baseball parties for my dad's teams, and summer cook-outs.
7. **VACATIONS** - Once a year we trekked to a historical site, an amusement park area or a trip for a new adventure.

I am the woman I am, due to all my mom and dad poured into me. I am forever grateful for the love and sacrifice my parents surrendered for my family and me.

The week my mom passed I was leading a devotional time with a group of ladies in the Diffusion Dance Company. I was reminded of the many attributes of God we so easily forget, which I took comfort in as I walked the 'Valley of the Shadow of Death.'

1. God is Immutable - Unchanging
2. Omni-present - Everywhere Present
3. Omniscient - All Knowing
4. Omnipotent - All Powerful
5. Sovereign - Over all

Let those amazing attributes sink in. It can change how you view the hard times during emotional roller coasters in life. Sometimes going barefoot in the dance is easier than trying to waltz in the wrong shoes.

I highly recommend the book, "Experiencing God: Knowing and Doing the Will of God," by Henry T. Blackaby. It is one of the most inspirational books I have ever read and has so positively impacted my dance. The two great takeaways:

1. God is Always at work. *(But Jesus replied, "My Father is always working and so am I. John 5:17)*
2. Join Him where He is at work

Sometimes I want to SLOW the dance down. Other times I want to rush through it at warp speed. Covid lockdowns was one of those times! As I look back over the last couple years of all the challenges, God made some good things come out of all the bad and blessed us in unexpected ways.

"Through the Lord's mercies we are not consumed, Because His compassions fail not.
They are new every morning; Great is Your faithfulness. 'The Lord is my portion,' says
my soul, 'Therefore I hope in Him!'" (Lamentations 3:22-24)

In the dance of sorrow, I cling to my God, His words in the Bible, and I am reminded from my journey – God is faithful!

23
Save the Last Dance for Me

When our church, Agape Fellowship Church, closed in 2017, we struggled with trying to find our way. We had only known God through the church, as Gary had left the steel mill to pursue ministry in 1986. The first church he pastored was five years later. God had fast-tracked us into ministry. We got caught up in the programs, meetings, church services and projects. After years of pushing, pushing and pushing more, we were in burnout.

We embarked on a journey by the leading of our pastors'-wives friends/spouses, who paid our way to attend SonScape Retreats in Lake Placid, New York. Many will remember this historic destination. This was the 1980's Olympic Center where the phrase, "Do you believe in miracles?!" resonated over the mic from the tension-filled battle between the Russian and United States Field Hockey Teams, resulting in the Gold USA victory! It was a seemingly David verses Goliath battle of iconic proportion which appeared out of reach at a time when all Americans needed hope.

SonScape provided a time of reflection, rest and intimacy with the Lord. During our stay we received advice from our counselors to consider closing the church. This was not what we wanted to hear, but knew it was what was needed for us to be healthier in our walk with the Lord and family. We had left our first love (Revelation 2:4), and we knew we needed to be out of ministry as much as the church needed us to step aside. We were crippling ourselves as well as others. God spared us and His people! I was completely unfamiliar with this kind of dance. Beth Moore said, *"Only the repentant know what it's like to dance with joy & gladness on broken legs."* Our legs had been broken! Well now. How do you dance with broken legs?

Through the next few years, we had to rediscover our love relationship with Jesus and put all of our Bible knowledge into action. Sometimes it was as if we were drowning and struggling to breathe as we navigated through a dry time like none other. Character can grow where there is conflict. While God was taking us *deeper in our dance with Him, we discovered this was our ultimate slow dance.*

Working through 6 part-time jobs now in our sixties, presented more challenges. Often, I thought - *I'd rather God take me home to Heaven before He takes My Dance.* Dance is therapy to me! As we navigate through this new season of life, the hurdles we face are challenging. God has been faithful to provide, strengthen and encourage us while going through all of the unknown. Covid, in many ways, became a blessing in disguise. It created another opportunity to take God at His Word and trust in deeper ways! When the finances were a real and very scary obstacle before us, I reminded my husband that we are not to live as paupers, but as Princes and Princesses.

Recently, the Supreme Court overturned Roe vs Wade after the ruling from 1973, almost 50 years ago! I know many may differ in opinion, but I am thankful the Justices took a stand for life. Many will not understand this, but I was a young woman who did not understand at the time of my pregnancy, that I was told a lie. I believed I was just carrying a fetus, a blob with no form. You have to remember; I was not a Christian and only went by hearsay and what friends told me. There was no internet - just people using abortion as a birth control method. I know what it's like to be *blinded*. I sympathize with people who can't see. I have been there! I have lived it. So, I don't condemn them, but rather try to share my story with them, whenever the door opens.

One of the greatest joys in my dance is the time spent with my grandchildren: Ocean, Isaiah, Azalea and Nova. They fill my tank even as they deplete it! A child keeps us seeing the world through a different lens – rose-colored, not judgmental, not racist, not restricted, not legalistic! Love knows no limitations. I love that my grands love me for who I am, not what I look like with all my warts and wrinkles! I love the quote by Sandra Bullock, "The rule is you have to dance a little bit in the morning before you leave the house, because it changes the way you walk out into the world." I hope my dance legacy will inspire my grandchildren to live life to the fullest and to dance every day! My Memaw-Grandma motto!

I want my life to ever be exuding the love of Christ and for Him to be my daily dance partner. I have tangoed with many others in life: selfishness, materialism, money and success. But I want to save the LAST DANCE for Jesus!

"I have seen everything that has been done under the sun, and behold, all is vanity and a chase after the wind." (Ecclesiastes 1:4)

24
Just Dance

One morning I received one of the most rewarding comments I could ever receive: "Cheryl, much gratitude to you for teaching Lauren excellent tap technique." Taryn, Lauren's mom, filled me in with where her lovely and talented daughter was performing. Lauren recently auditioned and was cast in Irving Berlin's White Christmas at the LaComedia Dinner Theater in Springboro, Ohio. How exciting to have former students making a difference through tap dance. It is a teacher's glory to hear your students continue on and excel in theater, musicals, audition for the Rockettes and become dance instructors themselves! You never know how your vocation will impact a child's or a dancer's life. The legacy lives on through what you instilled in them through the art of dance.

The thrill of performing on stage brings oodles of butterflies and immense anticipation. Some people are made for the stage! Others run far from it. Each person is created however God uniquely designed them.

And as a little sidenote, there is a phrase often used before a show - "Break a Leg." At a young age, I never understood what that meant. In case you still don't know what it means, in essence, it is wishing a person a good performance or good luck.

Sometimes as I walk up the stairwell to the studio, I wonder how much longer I will be able to teach. At 63, my body doesn't always cooperate with me. Even though I teach seven tap classes on a Thursday night back-to-back without a break, I am actually more energized by the end of the night than I am depleted!

I experience such deep fulfillment and internal joy as I watch the dancers grow through their metamorphosis from their first lesson to achieving their aspirations or their dreams. I have heard students say, "I have two left feet!" Not so! Even the most uncoordinated student can learn and be trained. I encourage them to JUST DANCE. We all grow together!

"I CAN'T!" Oh my!!! I hold my ears when a child says to me that they CAN'T! I tell them that hurts my ears!!! Miss Cheryl does not accept those words in class. I help them understand they CAN and we will work till they get it!

Recently, I was on Facebook and read a poem written by a dancer who attends Light of Life Performing Arts. I asked my friend, Robin, if I could use her daughter's poem in my book? I could not pen the expression of the feeling of freedom that dance brings as well as this young dancer has captured in her own words.

"Dear Dance"
Taylor Bair

"Dear Dance,

You have been my dream since I was little
From the Nutcracker to Sleeping Beauty
I knew it all, copying every move
A smile beaming from my face
Dancing to the Nutcracker soundtrack my mom bought for me
Sometimes even with my brother by my side
My mom started it all
For she had danced too
The old pictures and tapes
She sparked my love and passion for you
Through the thick and the thin

I could shut myself in a room and put on a song
Boom
A different world
My own world
I could do whatever I needed to
To express myself
To shake off anxiety
To rejoice
To mourn
Anything my heart desired
For when the song drifted through my ears, I let everything go

From the first time I heard a Nutcracker song
To now dancing on my toes
You have been with me always
And I will forever love you for that
You are such a joy to watch and perform
From the countless hours of practice
To the single hour for when I perform
I have worked so hard for you

The stage goes black, now is the time
We all run onto the stage
Waiting for the lights to brighten the stage
As I close my eyes I remember it's all for you
The stage comes to life and I see the audience
I dance my heart out until the lights go out once again
The sound of applause fills my ears
And I smile knowing that all my work has paid off
The pointe shoes which I got this year

I put them on slowly and carefully
The soft silk ribbons I feel as I cross them
The pain is a for sure
But it is all worth it for when I rise up onto my toes, the feeling is truly magical
You feel like you're floating
You feel like you can do anything

Misty Copeland
Michaela DePrince
Anna Pavlova
I knew everyone

For almost a decade now I have adored you
From my head to my toes
Every molecule in my body could not live without you
The feeling I get when I watch someone dance
With talent and grace
My heart goes 100 beats a minute
For you are so beautiful to watch and perform
You have grace and flow
Everything I could want
Every move I make

There are a billion things to think about
From the top of your head to the tips of your toes, from keeping your eyes up
To pointing you toes
It all runs through my mind
As I do that one single move
That perfect pirouette
Or that graceful glissade

The work is hard
But you get even better from it
That's just how it is
The more you stretch
The more flexible you get
The more you push your limits
The farther your limits get
The more you know the choreography
The more you can express yourself while doing the choreography
And the same is true with life
Work for your goals
Work towards getting better
Work towards pushing your limits farther and farther

You inspire and teach me every day
You taught me not to care about what other people think

You taught me to let go of things that were holding me down
But most importantly you taught me is to be me
Freedom

The best word to describe how I feel when I dance, The smell of sweat, pain, passion
Every single thing is worth it when I step on stage, You keep me motivated
You keep me passionate
You help me through the darkest of times
You help me rejoice through the best of times
My heart belongs to you

Yours truly ~ Taylor Bair"

The heart can beat through dance in ways that only those who have experienced it can understand. Try it! Take a class. Turn on your radio when no one is watching, grab your child/grandchild and twirl!

So . . . put on your dancing shoes. There is nothing more exhilarating. Just dance!

25
The Finale - Last Dance

At the end of a show, all of the actors and dancers, who have performed will assemble together on stage to take a bow. The Finale! Our Finale Dance will surely come unless Jesus returns for His church first! I am waiting for the trumpet sound; anyone else with me?

Many of us start out well, but finishing the race is not easy. A wise preacher, Dr. Harry E. Fletcher (Global Ambassador to Good News Jail & Prison Ministry), preached a message at our church anniversary: "It is not how you start, but how you finish! Finish well!" This quote was actually from President Will Culbertson, Moody Bible Institute. It stuck to me like glue.

As a Christian, I wait for the Ultimate dance. I cannot know if today will be my day when God calls me home. I know when that day comes, I will waltz right into my Savior's arms not feeling the sting of death. I will close my eyes; my heart will stop, and a brand-*new dance* will begin. Eternity.

CHOREOGRAPHY OF MY LAST DANCE

At my own "home-going" service, I would like to have these songs sung: "I'll Fly Away," "Oh, Happy Day" and Matt Redman's "10,000 Reasons." I do not want a somber event, but rather a joyous remembrance of how my life-dance touched others.

At the wake, I would love to have tap music and bright-colored balloons creating an event that is a celebration of joy! A happy, festive atmosphere with Big Band music and tap shoes everywhere – that's what it should be! A Dance Party! Whoo-hoo! Anyone who knows me at dance anticipates at the conclusion of every dance season to break out into a Dance Party with the song "Everybody Dance Now" ("Gonna Make You Sweat").

I hope my family, friends and students will always remember my deepest heart's desire: "It would please me most to be remembered as someone who loved life and danced and made the most of all God had for me each day!" This may all sound a little creepy to some, but at 63 years old, you begin to look at the road ahead and realize you are in the last quarter of your dance.

Sometimes I daydream of what Heaven will be like and wonder if we will dance there. I imagine the exuberance we will experience when we see Jesus face-to-face and I wonder, "how could there not be dancing in Heaven?"

Hearing the song "I Can Only Imagine" while riding down the country roads of York, Pennsylvania, I listened to the lyrics in a whole new way: "Will I dance for you, Jesus, or in awe of You be still?" Someone other than me has pondered this thought as well. Thanks, Mercy Me! Of course, we won't know until we reach the other side. But, if we do dance, I want my dance to hog-up at least a millennium in eternity! Sorry. Wait in line.

Martha Graham was quoted as saying, "Dance is the hidden language of the soul." Martha was a U.S. choreographer and dancer from 1894 – 1991. Her legacy and influence on modern dance over 70 years in American culture changed the way people perceived dance. In the 1994 documentary "The Dance Revealed," Martha said,

> *"I have spent all my life with dance and being a dancer. It's permitting life to use you in a very intense way. Sometimes it is not pleasant. Sometimes it is fearful. But, nevertheless, it is inevitable." (Wikipedia)*

It is inevitable in life that at some point we will deal with grief, mourning so deeply that we feel like we want to die along with the loved ones we lose. In reality, we don't really want to die – we want to be out of the pain that the loss inflicts.

I long to see my loved ones on the other side. As a child, my Grandmother Kyte (Florence) made several spiritual deposits into my young life. She introduced me to the organ and sweet hymns she played for me. I remember children's Bible storybooks as I sat on Grandmom's lap. She followed me to all my dance recitals as long as she could. I so look forward to her greeting me in Heaven. Grandmothers have a special place in your life. My Grandmother Carter left a legacy that changed the course of my life as well as many others. I can't wait to dance with my dad in Heaven - he could "cut a rug." My mom will be of sound mind – thank you Jesus! In Heaven I will see our other two children whom I have never met; one from the miscarriage and the other from the abortion. I have given them names that would be interchangeable for either gender: Kelly and Erin/Aaron. I look forward to them greeting me in Heaven.

There are others I am looking forward to meeting in Heaven: our granddaughters, Canon, Paisley and Hope, my dear friend, Flo, and so many dear sisters and brothers in the Lord who have preceded me to Heaven. Who are you looking forward to meeting in Heaven?

"The Secret of the Dance," a novel by author Susan Eileen Walker, a heartfelt novel about pursuing dreams following the character of Jeremy Applegate, a dancer who fled to New York for his lifelong dream of a career in dance, he shares with his niece, Remi, (also a dancer) the following:

> *"I think that a dancer should concentrate on dancing wherever she can, wherever she is. She should take part in every performance she can get into and build up her resume. Dancing in a performance arts high school might be nice, but you might lose something very important along the way. Stay here, study hard, dance and dance and dance, and enjoy life."*

That resonates in my heart! While here on earth, ". . . dance and dance and dance, and enjoy life!" I love it! People ask me, "When are you going to stop dancing?" My answer is always simple – "As long as my heart is beating, I will dance!"

Ann Voskamp wrote:

> *"The art of really celebrating life isn't about getting it right – but about receiving 'grace.' The sinners and the sick, the broken, the discouraged, the*

wounded and burdened – we are the ones who get to celebrate grace! Regardless of the mess of your life, if Christ is Lord of your life, then we are the celebrants out dancing in a wild rain of grace – because when it's all done and finished, all is well and Christ already said it was finished."

Again, it is inevitable that we will all experience death, unless the Lord raptures us out first. No one can cheat physical death. Dancing may be the hidden language of the soul, but as much as I love dance to the very core of my being, my soul longs for significantly more than dance. I long for Christ. And, as much as I have been able to express myself through dance and enjoy it on this side of eternity, it will dramatically pale in comparison to spending eternity with Christ.

Kelly Minter writes:

> *"So those who have faith are blessed with Abraham, who had faith. Our part is to be faithful; His part is to be a covenant God. It's a **sacred dance** no one quite understands this side of Heaven, yet we are invited to **dance** it anyway."*

So, when I enter into God's glory, this may sound a bit strange to some, but I will be in the presence of the Lord. What a great gettin' up day it will be! There may be those who will be solemn or sad at my "homegoing" service, but I want them to celebrate with me. This is my desired epitaph: *She walked with God, like Enoch (Genesis 5:24); she loved life and the One who gave it to her –Jesus, her Savior!* I will be in His presence safe and secure.

Life is short and this is not a dress rehearsal! We only get one life to live – not a re-do. I am not sure, in God's timeline, if we are in Act 1, Act 2, Intermission or the Finale. I want to be ready every day for Jesus' return, making the most of each opportunity God has planned. I said to my children when they walked out the front door to go to school – *"Make this the best day you can"* (we never know if it will be our last). I only verbalized the first part - the truth of the second part only being in my mind.

Jesus said, "the very hairs on your head are numbered" and the suffering Job of the Old Testament said, *"You have decided the length of our lives. You know how many months we will live."* So, dance like there's no tomorrow. If Jesus tarries and I don't hear a trumpet sound, I know I will pass from this life to eternal LIFE! No sting of eternal death - just a breath away from Heavenly bliss. I know I will glide into my Savior's Arms as I am Heaven-bound. Next . . . to dance in eternity!

Please plan to come and join me!
Let me know if this book was helpful in your journey, led you to Christ or challenged you to live a Life of Dance!

*Kelly Minter, The Living Room Series; Nehemiah – A Heart That Can Break; LifeWay Press, Nashville, TN; p 121